Theatre

Student Handbook

Dinos Aristidou

Foreword by
Mike Bindon

ista
Global learning through theatre

The International Schools Theatre Association
Lakeside Offices, The Old Cattle Market
Helston, Cornwall, TR13 0SR
United Kingdom

www.ista.co.uk

ISBN: 979-8-9869645-0-8

Printed in the United States of America

⊗ This paper meets the requirements of ANSI/NISO Z39.48-1992 (Permanence of Paper)

Cover design, book layout and illustrations by Red Curtain Studio (www.redcurtainstudio.com)

032023

Acknowledgements
Special thanks to the staff and students of the United World College of South East Asia, Singapore, for granting permission to use images from their theatre work in this publication.

The authors and publishers are grateful to the International Baccalaureate Organization (IBO) for permission to reproduce copyrighted extracts from the Diploma Programme *Theatre guide* (© IBO, 2022).

You should always check the current requirements of the DP theatre assessment tasks, since these might be subject to change during the life of the course. Your theatre teacher can access the most recent version of the *Theatre guide* via the IB's Programme Resource Centre (resources.ibo.org).

Dedication

Dinos Aristidou
1965 - 2023

A week prior to publishing this book we received the devastating news that our principal author and dear friend, Dinos Aristidou, had passed away.

Dinos was a passionate man of the arts, a gentle and loving human, and a courageous and innovative leader. His impact on global arts education has been extraordinary and his passion, guidance, wisdom and empathy have touched the lives of thousands of theatre students and teachers internationally.

His influence on both the International Baccalaureate's (IB) theatre course and on the International Schools Theatre Association (ISTA) is immeasurable.

He was central to the development of multiple IB arts courses over the past twenty years and his boundless creativity, infectious energy and incredible talent permeate every aspect of the IB's Diploma Programme theatre course.

His affiliation with ISTA dates back to its origins. Dinos inspired all those he worked with as an ISTA artist, workshop leader, and artistic director over the past three decades. He was recognised as an Honorary Life Member of the organisation following his tenure on the Board of Trustees and he commenced his most recent role as ISTA's Executive Director in 2022.

Dinos was truly an inspiration and he will continue to live on in what he has so generously shared with our community. This book is dedicated to his memory and it is our hope that a new generation of theatre-makers will be inspired to shine his light far and wide and to continue his visionary work of global learning through theatre.

We feel privileged to have been able to collaborate so closely with him in the creation of this unique resource for theatre students and will be forever grateful for the insight, joy and love he brought to this book and to our lives.

Mike Bindon

On behalf of The International Baccalaureate

Liane Campbell

On behalf of The ISTA Board of Trustees

About the authors

Dinos Aristidou is a writer, international teaching and learning consultant and theatre-maker. He has worked as a member of the International Baccalaureate's (IB) theatre development team for many years and was curriculum manager for the review of the Middle Years Programme *Arts guide*. He is currently Executive Director of ISTA.

Mike Bindon is an international arts curriculum developer and filmmaker. He taught theatre and film in secondary schools and currently works as Arts Curriculum Manager for the IB in The Hague, The Netherlands, where he oversees the development of the Diploma Programme (DP) theatre and film courses. He also runs his own video and creative media production studio.

About ISTA

The International Schools Theatre Association (ISTA) specialises in global learning through theatre. It is a UK-based charity, founded in 1978, providing transformative learning experiences for educators and young people worldwide.

ISTA creates communities of learning, working closely with a large number of member schools around the world. It is the IB's exclusive global provider of face-to-face teacher training for the DP theatre course, offering workshops at all levels for DP teachers. ISTA also runs learning experiences for DP theatre students around the world.

ISTA believes in the unique power of theatre and the arts to connect, develop, transform and empower people to become global learners and active members of their own communities and the world.

ISTA offers a range of resources, workshops and theatre experiences for DP theatre students and teachers. Please visit www.ista.co.uk for more information and to subscribe to ISTA's mailing list.

A note for teachers

This handbook has been created to accompany, supplement and reinforce the DP theatre course developed by the teacher. It has been created with the idea that each student in your class is issued with or obtains their own individual copy that they can personalize and write in.

You can use this handbook in a variety of different ways to support, augment and enrich the delivery of your theatre course.

- **As a student's journal:** It can be used as a student's theatre journal together with a digital or paper notebook. It provides space and guided activities for students to record their ideas, processes and learning. It also offers prompts for reflection and tips for success.

- **For differentiated learning:** Different students work at a different pace and have different needs. This handbook can be used as a source of activities for the differentiated classroom—giving some students activities to focus on while the rest of the class catches up, giving students who need more guidance additional activities to enhance their learning and/or providing students who need to be stretched with additional challenges.

- **For teachers teaching two grades together:** Some teachers are required to teach two different DP theatre year groups/grades together. This handbook provides one group of students with activities to work on while you tend to the other group. This is also particularly helpful during assessment when you will be conducting individual meetings with final year students to offer guidance, to supervise or to record their work.

- **For independent learning:** There will be occasions when the students need to work independently of you. This may be homework, when they are unable to attend the class, when the class is being supervised by another teacher and/or when students are working remotely. The handbook provides you with the opportunity to set work from the suggested activities for such occasions.

- **As revision before embarking on assessment tasks:** The handbook is a useful tool for revision. Each chapter may be used as a reminder or an introduction to the assessment tasks towards the end of the course. Each chapter takes students through processes outlined in the guide and recommended for assessment. They offer students a reminder of the criteria, top tips and insights into what the examiner wants to see.

- **As a resource and inspiration:** You can use the suggested activities and exercises alongside your own to develop a particular unit, add a different dimension to your lessons or as inspiration for new approaches to the teaching of the course.

Contents

6: Performing theatre theory and the solo theatre piece (HL only)

Appendices

Foreword

It is with great pleasure that I write this foreword in my capacity as Curriculum Manager for the International Baccalaureate's (IB) Diploma Programme (DP) theatre course. I consider that this handbook is long overdue, and I have no doubt that it will be eagerly welcomed by students and teachers alike. This handbook is the outcome of a decade's work in collaboratively developing and refining the IB's theatre course alongside an inspiring group of international educators.

The IB theatre course is built on the belief that the arts play a central role in the development of young learners, and that through collaborative exploration, creation and play, a wealth of irreplaceable skills and competencies can be acquired and honed. Theatre has the power to unite communities, strengthen shared identities and transcend cultural barriers. In a time when young people are so heavily influenced by the digital, theatre continues to offer a physically grounding and spiritually connecting experience. A place of lived knowledge, of somatic exploration and real-time collaboration. I am thrilled to see this student handbook delivering this core vision of our *Theatre guide* directly to students.

I am extremely grateful to Mike Pasternak, our current Chief Examiner for theatre, who so elegantly shared with me in my early days as a curriculum manager what he considered to be the fundamental role of the IB theatre curriculum. It should offer students the opportunity to "open the door" on the rich and dynamic array of theatre experiences that exist in the world, where they should be encouraged to seek cultural insight, creative inspiration and transformational self-discovery. This handbook has been written with this spirit in mind, as an experience that not only takes students into the world of the *Theatre guide*, but which hopefully opens the door to the unlimited potential of theatre in the world.

Every IB theatre educator involved in the development of the subject is passionate about the course being a practical, dynamic, and imaginative subject for our students to study, and I am delighted that this handbook is so richly underpinned by these principles. Dinos Aristidou has superbly composed an imaginative road map for students to navigate the theatre course at their own pace, be it as a resource for those individuals who are working solo, or for those students who are seeking to enrich their existing taught course with additional inspiration and support.

I have had the pleasure of collaborating with Dinos since my very first encounter with the IB in 2012, and I have greatly valued his creativity, energy and wisdom—all of which he has instilled into the exciting activities, engaging exercises and rich resources presented here. It has been a joy to work alongside him on this venture.

I am indebted to Liane Campbell and the ISTA Board of Trustees for fulfilling my ambition to create this resource for our IB theatre students, and for their patience and perseverance as we jointly navigated the world of commercial publishing. A massive amount of work has gone into producing this resource and I am truly appreciative of ISTA's willingness to invest so deeply in supporting our theatre learners.

ISTA's mission for enabling young people to have meaningful access to the arts so closely aligns with the aspirations of the IB to develop inquiring, knowledgeable and caring young people who help to create a better and more peaceful world through education that builds intercultural understanding and respect.

I am certain that students will find this resource to be immensely valuable and easily accessible, and hope that they find inspiration and joy in developing their skills while responding to the imaginative activities and exercises. I wish them every success on their IB theatre journey!

Mike Bindon
Curriculum Manager for Diploma Progamme theatre
International Baccalaureate

We would like to take this opportunity to thank the following individuals for their valuable contributions and support during the development of this handbook: Liane Campbell, Nita Dewse, Rachel Love, Fenella Kelly, Keriann O'Rourke, Anna Parr, Mike Pasternak, Susie Shreeve and Sam Smart.

1. Welcome to DP theatre

> Theatre is a dynamic, collaborative and live art form. It is a practical subject that encourages discovery through practical inquiry, experimentation, risk taking and the presentation of ideas to others.
>
> (*Theatre guide*, 2022).

Introduction

The DP theatre course is an exciting and engaging course, and this handbook has been specifically developed to help you navigate the wonderfully creative challenges that lie ahead as you begin your journey as a student of DP theatre.

The theatre course encourages you to work as an inquisitive and imaginative artist, requiring you to transform ideas into action and to communicate these to an audience. Through the activities contained in this handbook, you will explore theatre across time, place and culture to discover and engage with a variety of different theatrical forms, practices and processes. It is our hope that you will emerge from your theatre course as a more confident, imaginative, creative and collaborative theatre-maker.

While the explorations and exercises contained in this handbook will help to prepare you for the demands of the DP theatre assessment tasks, they are also designed to help you develop as an ethically responsible and internationally minded theatre-maker, embodying the values of the IB's learner profile.

This introductory chapter will provide you with an overview of the theatre course, guide you through each of the chapters that follow, and explain how to use this handbook for maximum success in your theatre work.

The chapter is arranged as follows.

1.1   Purpose of this handbook
1.2   The theatre course at a glance
1.3   How your work is assessed
1.4   The theatre journal
1.5   The DP core
1.6   Working with this handbook in practice

1.1 Purpose of this handbook

This handbook is intended to provide practical support for students of the DP theatre course. It has been designed to take you through the four syllabus areas of the theatre course and each of the four accompanying assessment tasks. As such, it offers an invaluable support and accompaniment to the course you are undertaking at your school.

> **Access to the Theatre guide**
> All official information regarding the theatre course, including the specific requirements of each assessment task and criteria, can be found in the Theatre guide (first assessment 2024). Your theatre teacher or your school's DP coordinator will be able to provide you with a copy of this important document.

Direct extracts from the *Theatre guide* are presented in grey boxes throughout the handbook. These are titled:

What the guide says

These extracts present the formal requirements of each assessment task and are intended to draw your attention to the important details regarding the assessment work that is submitted to the IB.

> **Top tip**
> Key recommendations, useful theatre terminology, helpful tips and opportunities for reflection are highlighted in boxes like this throughout the handbook.

Each chapter contains practical exercises and activities, many of them with space for you to respond, capture your ongoing work, your developing ideas and your reflections.

All of the activities have been designed so that you can work on your own, with a partner, in a small group or with your whole class. You can use them at school, at home or in any other appropriate setting.

1.2 The theatre course at a glance

The syllabus areas
The theatre course is comprised of four syllabus areas. Three of these areas are for both standard level (SL) and higher level students (HL), and one is for HL students only.

Staging play texts	Exploring world theatre traditions	Collaboratively creating original theatre	Performing theatre theory (HL only)

Staging play texts: This area of the syllabus addresses the transformation of play texts into action. Students examine the ways in which ideas are presented by playwrights in play texts and the ways in which performance and production elements can be used to bring text to life.

Exploring world theatre traditions: This area of the syllabus addresses the authentic exploration of world theatre traditions through academic and practical research. Students inquire into and physically explore world theatre traditions, performance conventions and performance material from those traditions in order to acquire a deeper understanding and appreciation of the traditions through the body and/or voice.

Collaboratively creating original theatre: This area of the syllabus addresses the collaborative development and performance of original theatre. Students formulate intentions for theatre-making and examine the ways in which these intentions can be effectively realized through the collaborative creation of original performance work inspired by a starting point. This is then prepared and presented to an audience.

Performing theatre theory (HL only): This area of the syllabus addresses the exploration of aspects of theatre theory and the ways in which theory can inform performance. Students research at least one theatre theorist, identify an aspect of their theory and apply this to create and present a solo performance piece to an audience.

The assessment tasks

The learning in each of these core syllabus areas is assessed by its own distinct assessment task. These assessment tasks are: the production proposal; the research presentation; the collaborative project; the solo theatre piece (HL only).

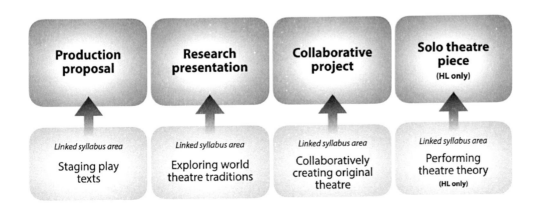

Assessment task	SL	HL
Production proposal Students at SL and HL choose a published play text they have not previously studied and formulate a vision for the design and theoretical staging of the entire play text for an audience. These ideas are presented in the form of a proposal. Each student submits the following. 1. A production proposal (a maximum of 12 pages of written text and images, with written text not exceeding 4,000 words) plus a list of all sources used	30%	20%
Research presentation Students at SL and HL plan, deliver and video record an individual research presentation (15 minutes maximum) in which they provide evidence of their academic and practical exploration and learning of a world theatre tradition they have not previously studied. Each student submits the following. 1. A video recording of the student's research presentation (15 minutes maximum) 2. A list of all sources cited and any additional resources used by the student during the presentation	30%	20%
Collaborative project Students at SL and HL collaboratively create and perform an original piece of theatre (lasting 7–10 minutes maximum) created from a starting point of their choice. The piece is presented to an audience as a fully realized production. Each student submits the following. 1. A project report (a maximum of 10 pages of written text and images, with written text not exceeding 4,000 words) plus a list of all sources used 2. A video recording of the final piece (7–10 minutes maximum)	40%	25%
Solo theatre piece (HL only) Students at HL research a theatre theorist they have not previously studied, identify an aspect(s) of theory and create and present a solo theatre piece (lasting 4–7 minutes maximum) that demonstrates the practical application of this theory to a theatre piece for an audience. Each student submits the following. 1. A report (2,500 words maximum) plus a list of all primary and secondary sources cited 2. A continuous unedited video recording of the whole solo theatre piece (4–7 minutes maximum)		35%

1.3 How your work is assessed

Assessment criteria

Each of the assessment tasks in the theatre course is assessed through criteria. These criteria are presented in each chapter and are individually addressed through various practical activities. You will find the criteria and weightings (how many marks each individual criterion is worth) presented as follows.

	Production proposal	Marks	Total
A	Ideas and intentions	8	
B	The proposed design	4	20
C	The proposed staging of one moment of the play	8	

The individual strands of criteria for each area of the assessment task are presented in a box. This also tells you where the examiner will look for evidence that you have met the requirements of the task.

> **Production proposal assessment criteria**
> **Criterion C: The proposed staging of one moment of the play**
> Evidence: production proposal
>
> i. To what extent does the student explain how they would use **performance** elements to effectively create tension, emotion, atmosphere and/or meaning ("TEAM") in one specific moment they have chosen to stage?
> ii. To what extent does the student explain how they would use **production** elements to effectively create tension, emotion, atmosphere and/or meaning ("TEAM") in one specific moment they have chosen to stage

At the end of each chapter you will also find guidance as to what the examiner wants to see.

There are four levels of attainment for each criterion. Each level descriptor in the markband hierarchy has its own command term that defines what you need to do to get marks in that level.

You will need to familiarize yourself with the command term definitions, as well as the performance and evaluative terms—all of which are provided overleaf/opposite/below. Make sure you understand each of them and know how they apply to your theatre work. You might want to check with your teacher, who may have examples of what each of these assessment terms looks like in action in the work of students from previous years.

> Being aware of how you will be assessed is key. This will help you to determine what you need to do to reach the highest level of attainment.

Definition: Criteria strands
Each assessment criterion has individual elements, or strands, that you need to address in your theatre work. Each strand is worth 4 marks. It is important, therefore, to pay attention to what each strand requires and to ensure that your final assessment work addresses each strand.

Top tip
It is important that you pay close attention to what each criterion is asking for, as this will have a direct impact on the marks you are awarded for each area in the final assessments.

Definition: Command term
Command terms are words that have a precise assessment definition and directly link to an achievement level. Examiners use these words to describe work they are marking. The more challenging the expectations of the command term, the higher number of marks are associated with it.

Hierarchy of command terms for theatre

Markband level	Command term	Description of student attainment
1	List	The student's work provides a sequence of brief answers with little or no attempt at explanation.
2	Outline	The student's work provides a brief account or summary, but this is underdeveloped.
3	Describe	The student's work provides a detailed account.
4	Explain	The student's work provides a thorough and detailed account, including insightful reasons or causes.

Hierarchy of performance terms for theatre

Markband level	Performance term	Description of student attainment
1	Limited	The student's work is constrained, demonstrating a restricted capability.
2	Moderate	The student's work is partially adept, demonstrating some capability, but not necessarily producing results as intended.
3	Competent	The student's work is convincing, demonstrating a capable level of skill and partially producing results as intended.
4	Effective	The student's work is compelling, demonstrating a high proficiency of skill and producing results that were intended.

Hierarchy of evaluative terms for theatre

Markband level	Evaluative term	Description of student attainment
1	Comment	The student provides a series of brief statements about their work with little or no attempt at evaluation.
2	Consider	The student provides a summary of their opinion of the work undertaken.
3	Appraise	The student provides a detailed judgement of the work undertaken, with some consideration of the strengths and/or limitations.
4	Evaluate	The student provides an insightful assessment of the qualities of the work undertaken, including a balance of strengths and limitations.

> For your ease of reference, the full criteria for all four theatre assessment tasks are presented in the "Appendices" at the back of this handbook.

1.4 The theatre journal

The *Theatre guide* requires that, from the beginning of the course, and at regular intervals, you maintain a theatre journal. The theatre journal is intended to be your own record of your studies of the DP theatre course. It should be used to record the following.

➤ Approaches to inquiry and research
➤ Creative ideas
➤ Creative processes
➤ Development of ideas through practical experimentation
➤ Evaluations and reflections
➤ Experiences of working as a creator, designer, director and performer
➤ Feedback received and action taken in response
➤ Ongoing evaluations of your own work and development
➤ Personal challenges and successes
➤ Responses to diverse starting points, play texts, theatre traditions and theatre theorists
➤ Responses to live theatre productions as a spectator
➤ Skills acquisition and development

Using this handbook to support your theatre journal

This handbook has been designed to fulfil some of the aspects of a journal by offering spaces for you to record your ongoing work. You will, however, also need to find other ways of recording your learning to go alongside this handbook. This can be through handwritten notes in a notebook, through the creation of digital documents and media files or via an alternative approach that works well for you.

1.5 The DP core

As well as the subjects that you have chosen to study as part of your diploma, all DP students are also required to fulfil the requirements of the DP core. The DP core is made up of three important course elements—creativity, activity, service (CAS), the extended essay (EE) and theory of knowledge (TOK).

This section addresses links between the theatre course and each area of the core in turn.

Creativity, activity, service

CAS is designed to involve you in a range of activities alongside your academic studies throughout the DP. The three strands of CAS are as follows.

● Creativity—arts, and other experiences that involve creative thinking
● Activity—physical exertion contributing to a healthy lifestyle
● Service—an unpaid and voluntary exchange that has a learning benefit for the student

CAS is a really important feature of the DP as it requires you to engage and connect with others and contributes to the IB's mission to create a better and more peaceful world through intercultural understanding and respect.

The practical, creative and collaborative nature of theatre perfectly complements the ethos of CAS.

You can use your theatre course to inspire CAS projects and initiatives as well as using your CAS experiences to inspire your theatre work. It is important, however, to remember that anything that is part of your theatre course cannot be counted as CAS. Likewise, anything that you count as CAS **cannot be part of your theatre course or the theatre assessment tasks.**

Here are some possible ways that you could use the theatre syllabus as an inspiration for CAS.

➤ Form a group and put on an evening of theatre for a class, for the school or for a community audience.
➤ Create and present pieces of theatre to address school, local or global issues.
➤ Put on a production to raise money for charity.
➤ Run a theatre workshop or theatre activities in a particular community.
➤ Run a theatre workshop or run a theatre class for younger students.
➤ Start a theatre club at your school or in the community.
➤ Create/stage a piece of theatre to tour to community settings where there is little access to theatre.
➤ Collaborate with charities to create workshops or pieces of theatre.
➤ Create pieces of theatre to bring areas of the curriculum to life.
➤ Support or take part in a community production or a school production.

Extended essay

The EE, including the world studies EE, offers you the opportunity to investigate a topic of special interest, in the form of a 4,000-word piece of independent research.

You will choose your EE from the list of available DP subjects for the assessment session. It is normally based on one of your six chosen subjects, or in the case of the inter-disciplinary world studies essay, two of your subjects. It leads to a major piece of formally presented, structured writing, in which ideas and findings are communicated in a reasoned and coherent manner, appropriate to the subject or subjects chosen. An authentic learning experience, it provides you with an opportunity to engage in personal research on a topic of choice, under the guidance of a supervisor. The EE gives you a taste of the independent research and writing skills expected at university.

An EE in theatre offers you the opportunity to develop a focused research question in an area of theatre that interests you. You will then undertake independent research into this theatre topic and present your research and explorations in an imaginative and critical way in the form of an essay.

A theatre EE has its own set of criteria that can be found in the *Extended essay guide*.

Theory of knowledge

The TOK course examines the nature of knowledge and how we know what we claim to know. It is a course that is fundamentally about critical thinking and inquiry into the process of knowing rather than about learning a specific body of knowledge.

TOK encourages you to analyse knowledge claims and explore questions about the construction of knowledge. It emphasizes connections between areas of shared knowledge and links them to personal knowledge so that an individual becomes more aware of their own perspectives. It also encourages you to reflect critically on your own beliefs and assumptions and on how they might differ from those of others.

The theatre course complements the TOK ethos by revealing interdisciplinary connections and encouraging you to reflect on and question your own bases of knowledge. It is also an opportunity to explore individual and cultural perspectives related to the arts. By exploring theatre processes, practices and traditions, you are also able to gain an understanding of the interdependent nature of knowledge and—as much of theatre is collaborative—shared knowledge.

Below are some prompts to help you make connections between theatre, the arts and other areas of knowledge.

- **Are some types of knowledge more useful than others?** For a performer, what is the difference between intuitive knowledge and theoretical knowledge?
- **What counts as good evidence for a claim?** How do we provide evidence for the impact of an arts experience on an audience?
- **To what extent is certainty attainable?** How certain can I be that my intentions for a piece of theatre are successful?
- **Are some types of knowledge less open to interpretation than others?** Is academic research more valuable than researching through the body?
- **Can new knowledge change established values or beliefs?** To what extent is it theatre's role to challenge the way we view the world?
- **What is the relationship between personal experience and knowledge?** How do I use my experience of unfamiliar theatre traditions to inform the areas of theatre I already know?
- **What is the relationship between knowledge and culture?** What do we discover about a culture through the study of its theatre?
- **What role do experts play in influencing our consumption or acquisition of knowledge?** How do theatre critics influence the development of contemporary theatre?
- **How can we distinguish between knowledge, belief and opinion?** How do we judge a piece of theatre?
- **How is current knowledge shaped by its historical development?** How does theatre theory evolve from and react against the theatre that has gone before it?

The IB learner profile
The IB learner profile underpins not only all of the IB's subjects but also all of its programmes. The learner profile aims to develop learners who are:

See p. 139 for full details of the IB learner profile.

These attributes reflect the spirit with which you should approach your theatre course and theatre explorations—with the ultimate purpose of strengthening and deepening these characteristics. This handbook and its activities have been created with this overarching goal in mind. As you work your way through the handbook, you may want to reflect on which characteristics of the learner profile each syllabus area and assessment task aims to enhance.

1.6 Working with this handbook in practice

After this introductory chapter, you will find that the rest of this handbook is divided into the following chapters.

Chapter 2: Being a theatre-maker

Chapter 3: Staging play texts and the production proposal

Chapter 4: Exploring world theatre traditions and the research presentation

Chapter 5: Collaboratively creating original theatre and the collaborative project

Chapter 6: Performing theatre theory and the solo theatre piece (HL only)

Appendices: Assessment criteria

The next chapter, "Being a theatre-maker", is the perfect place to start your theatre journey, as this chapter takes you through the fundamentals of being an IB theatre-maker. It introduces you to key theatre ideas and gives you understandings of areas of the course that appear across the syllabus. This will help you to develop your skills both as an IB theatre-maker and as a learner.

Chapters 3–6 can be studied in any order. If you are working through the whole handbook in class, your teacher might decide on the order. If you are working alone, you can decide the order based on your interests. Alternatively, you might choose to work through a chapter on an area of the course you are finding particularly challenging and want to explore further. The chapters are also a good way to revise before beginning an assessment task.

Each chapter begins with an introduction that gives you an overview of what is included. The chapters end with a focus on the assessment task, what you have to do, the criteria and what the examiner wants to see. A final recap summarizes what you have covered in that chapter.

Approaching the exercises
The DP theatre course is a practical subject and values the importance of **experimentation**, **play** and **learning through action**.

This handbook has therefore been developed with this important feature in mind. You will find a wealth of practical exercises and activities that are designed to develop your skills and understandings. These are activities that you can do in addition to the many activities you will be doing with your teacher on the course.

The practical exercises in each chapter follow a particular order so it is best to do them in sequence. Some activities build on and develop the work done in a previous activity.

Alongside the practical activities you will also find written activities to help you to record your reflections, your creative ideas and your learning. In some instances, you may be asked to audio record or video record some of your work in progress. With this in mind, you will need to have a device—such as a mobile phone, tablet or laptop—handy so that you are able to make the most of these opportunities.

This handbook offers you strategies that will help you with your assessment tasks. It is important to note that the activities you undertake in this handbook are not intended to target every requirement of the theatre assessment tasks, as your final assessment work in each area will be undertaken under specific conditions set by your teacher. The best way to think about this handbook is as a direct route into the theatre course with signposted activities and resources to help you develop the essential skills that will be required to navigate each official assessment task.

This handbook has been written as a space for experimentation and play as well as a guide to success. We hope it develops your skills and understandings, inspires you, and provides you with a map of your learning.

Enjoy the adventure!

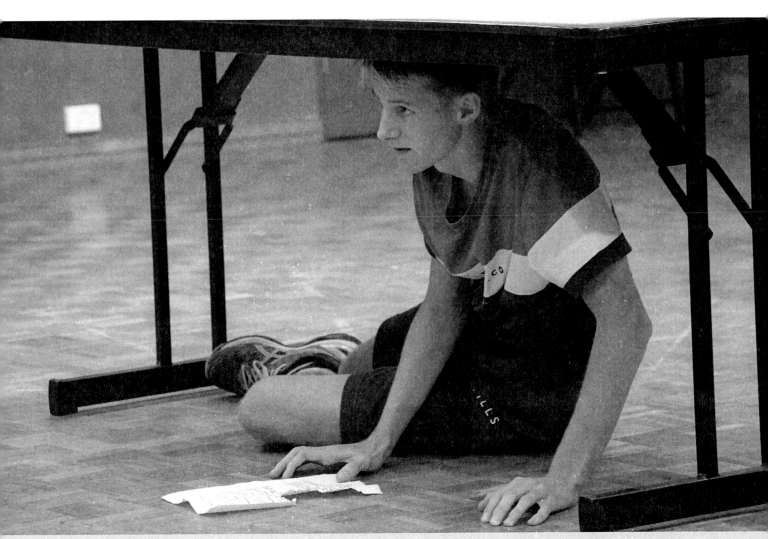

2

2. Being a theatre-maker

For all activities in this section you can either work individually, in pairs or in small groups.

Theatre course fundamentals

There are certain aspects of the course you can think of as the fundamentals that are useful for all the syllabus areas and assessment tasks. Understanding these will really help you with all your explorations and work as they cut across most of the assessments and are useful guidelines, even when they are not explicitly mentioned in the guide.

These fundamental areas are as follows:

2.1   The theatre-making process
2.2   The four theatre-making perspectives
2.3   Staging: Performance spaces
2.4   Staging: Performance elements
2.5   Staging: Production elements
2.6   Theatre-maker intentions and responsible theatre-making
2.7   Moments of tension, emotion, atmosphere and/or meaning ("TEAM")

2.1 The theatre-making process

There are many different approaches to theatre-making. This is dependent on a wide range of factors that include not only theatre's cultural, social and historical context, but also economics and ideas regarding what theatre is and what it is for. It is also determined by the type of theatre that is being made and the people who are making it.

The *Theatre guide* presents a theatre-making process that is made up of four stages. These four stages are important because they also follow the process of each of your assessment tasks. Each stage in the process should inform how you explore theatre and how you plan, prepare and present your assessments.

> **Reflection point**
> *How are theatre and theatre-making defined by where you are?* Look into how theatre is made in the place where you live. Is this different to how theatre is made in your school? What does the creation of theatre tell us about the society in which it is being made? How has theatre-making changed over time and what has instigated these changes?

Inquiring > Developing > Presenting > Evaluating

Inquiring
Inquiring focuses on research, on asking questions, on being curious, on examining how theatre is created, on exploring play texts, theatre traditions, theatre theorists, live theatre, and on learning through traditional academic research as well as through physical experimentation and play.

Developing

Developing focuses on the development of a piece of theatre or a piece of work, from its beginning to its final draft. This is the stage of drafting, repeating, experimenting and rehearsing. It includes the discovery of new ideas and the creation of new work. In this stage feedback from others is also really useful as it helps you to develop your work further. In this stage you will not only be developing your theatre work but also developing yourself, gaining the skills needed to fulfil the requirements of the work and succeed in the assessment tasks.

Presenting

Presenting is the moment when theatre work is presented as a finished product and shown to someone else. This is often what we call "the moment of realization of a work". In other words, when an idea is "made real". This might be a piece of theatre, a portfolio, a proposal, a presentation or a report. Though often, in theatre, we can continue working on something over lengthy periods of time, it is also important to decide when something needs to be ready by and to give ourselves a deadline.

Knowing that an end point has been decided focuses the mind, makes the process richer and helps us to plan our time better. Theatre relies on meeting deadlines; you cannot tell an audience on opening night that something is not quite ready. Careful planning, good organization and clear aims are all part of theatre making.

Evaluating

Evaluating is a key feature of any theatre process or indeed any learning process more generally. This stage involves self-reflection, looking back at your work, looking back to original intentions, listening to what others have to say about the work and figuring out what you need to do next. There are three parts to it:

> **1) Reflection**
> This is the moment when you stop, look at and consider what you are doing, why you are doing it and how you are doing it.
>
> **2) Judgement**
> This is the moment when, based on your observations and reflections, you judge the extent to which your original intentions (what you set out to do) have been achieved and your ideas have been expressed. It is also when you consider the extent to which the processes and approaches you have used are the best ones for what you are trying to achieve.
>
> **3) Planning**
> After appraising what is working well and what needs to be changed, developed or modified, the planning phase is initiated to propose the next steps for moving forward.

Top tip
Theatre relies on meeting deadlines. When preparing to present theatre it is good to know that an end point has been decided. This helps those involved to focus their minds, makes the process richer and helps us to plan our time better.

Top tip
The word **value** is the root word of **evaluation**, so it is useful to think of evaluation as the process of deciding whether something is of value, worth maintaining and using again in the future or whether it should be discarded or abandoned. This process is useful for your development as a learner and as a young artist.

Further research
Carry out some research into different systems and frameworks for evaluation and choose some that you think may help you to evaluate your theatre work.

Activity

The theatre-making processes
- Look at each of the four stages of the theatre-making process and think of yourself as an inquirer, developer, presenter, and evaluator. Using the spaces overleaf, write a list of skills and characteristics that you think belong with each of these.

  For example, *"An inquirer needs to be inquisitive, to ask questions, to have research skills"*.

An **inquirer** needs:

A **developer** needs:

A **presenter** needs:

An **evaluator** needs:

Reflection point
If you were designing a theatre course, what would you have as the different stages of theatre-making? What order would you put them?

Creating a piece of theatre based on the ideas of a theatre theorist

Creating and performing an original piece of theatre

Exploring an unfamiliar theatre tradition

Directing and designing a play text

The four artistic roles

- Looking back at the skills and characteristics you listed in the previous activity, adopt a different physical position for each of these showing you inquiring, developing, presenting and evaluating. Capture these as selfies or ask a partner to take them.
- Consider each of the different syllabus areas of the theatre course and think about how the theatre-making process applies to them. Using the chart opposite, draw a diagram for each one of these areas to show what is involved in each stage of the process. For example, in "Creating and performing an original piece of theatre", inquiring involves thinking about what a play might be about and deciding what starting point will inspire your work.

  Your diagrams should freely and creatively show the dynamic nature of the different stages of the theatre-making process. For example, in "Exploring an unfamiliar theatre tradition" you might begin with inquiry and then go into developing your ideas and trying out new ideas and then back to inquiry to research further. Share and discuss.

2.2 The four theatre-making perspectives

Theatre-making is a collaborative process, bringing together different people with diverse skills to work together to make theatre. Roles and responsibilities for the various aspects of theatre-making vary from culture to culture and are often dependent on the nature of the theatre being created and the status theatre has in that particular cultural context.

The *Theatre guide* defines four artistic roles through which to explore the course. These are **creator, director, designer and performer.** These roles offer a useful perspective through which to approach your work and to focus your learning in theatre.

Creator: A creator is someone who makes original theatre from scratch.

Director: A director is someone who is responsible for the stage action in a piece of theatre. A director makes decisions about what happens in a performance space and considers the overall experience for an audience.

Designer: A designer is someone who is responsible for the look and feel of a piece of theatre. The designer makes decisions about scenic and technical elements and considers the specific effect these elements will have on an audience in support of a director's vision.

Performer: A performer is someone who uses their body and/or voice to create stage action as part of a piece of theatre that is presented to an audience.

Each of the assessment tasks requires you to adopt one or more of these perspectives to complete the task and to learn about theatre and theatre-making. Understanding and developing the skills related to each of these will guide your explorations of the syllabus areas as well as providing you with the tools you need for each of your final assessments.

Further research
Carry out some research to identify someone in your community who professionally works in one of these roles. What can you find out about their work and their skills?

- Research each of the following artistic theatre-making roles and explore the necessary responsibilities and skills related to each one.

  - ☑ Creator
  - ☑ Designer
  - ☑ Director
  - ☑ Performer

- Record the findings of your research using the chart overleaf.

A **creator** is responsible for:

The skills required to carry out the responsibilities of a **creator** include:

A **designer** is responsible for:

The skills required to carry out the responsibilities of a **designer** include:

A **director** is responsible for:

The skills required to carry out the responsibilities of a **director** include:

A **performer** is responsible for:

The skills required to carry out the responsibilities of a **performer** include:

The four perspectives

- Consider each of the following areas of theatre-making below and write some notes on how you think each of the artists would approach the staging of an original piece of theatre or an existing play text from the perspective of their roles.

Creator

Designer

Creating and staging an original piece of theatre

Director

Performer

Creator

Designer

Staging an existing play text or other existing material

Director

Performer

Linking the theatre processes and the perspectives

The theatre-making processes are common to all four of the perspectives but for each artistic role, the approach is slightly different. Inquiring as a performer, for example, is different to inquiring as a director.

Activity

The processes and perspectives

- Complete the following, then share it with a partner and discuss which perspectives you think differ the most and which are the most similar.

Inquiring for a creator involves ...

Inquiring for a designer involves ...

Inquiring for a director involves ...

Inquiring for a performer involves ...

Developing for a creator involves ...

Developing for a designer involves ...

Developing for a director involves ...

Developing for a performer involves ...

A creator presents ...

A designer presents ...

A director presents ...

A performer presents ...

A creator evaluates ...

A designer evaluates ...

A director evaluates ...

A performer evaluates ...

Reflection point

What are your existing strengths in theatre? Which areas do you most want to develop further? Considering each of the perspectives (creating, designing, directing, performing) draw four circles on some large chart paper showing, through the size of each circle, what you consider to be your own strongest areas of skill and experience. The larger the circle the greater your personal skill set and experience.

List the skills you feel you already have in each circle, related to each perspective. Around the outside of each circle, write what skills you hope to develop during the DP theatre course relating to each perspective.

2.3 Staging: Performance spaces

Theatre can be made anywhere and can be performed anywhere.

The performance space is what we call the space where a piece of theatre takes place. It plays a really important role because it determines so many aspects of the production. It is central to how the audience experiences a piece of theatre, the size of the audience, the way a theatre-maker is going to stage the piece and the resources that are needed. Your approach to creating, designing, directing and performing will differ depending on the performance space you will be working in.

Of course, anywhere can be a performance space and theatrical performances come in all shapes and sizes. In recent years, theatre has been presented not only in places purpose built for performance but also in innovative and unusual spaces. All theatre-makers are responsible for how the space is arranged and used, where the audience is located and what theatrical tools are used to shape the audience's experience of the piece of theatre. The task of each of the four artistic perspectives is also to decide where the focus of the audience's attention needs to be at any particular moment and what artistic choices they will make to ensure this happens.

Below are some examples of common performance space layouts.

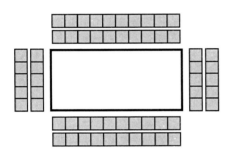

In the round or **arena**
A theatre space in which the audience completely surrounds the stage.

Thrust
A theatre space in which the stage is extended so that the audience surrounds it on three sides.

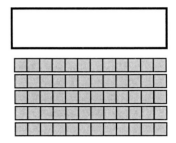

Proscenium arch or **end-on**
A theatre space in which the stage is at one end with the audience seated in front facing the stage.

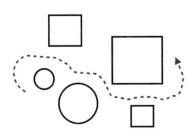

Promenade
A theatre space without fixed seating. This allows the standing audience to intermingle with the performers and to follow the focal point of the action to different parts of the space.

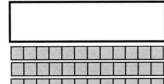

Traverse
A theatre space in which the audience seating is predominantly on two sides of the stage, facing towards each other. This layout is also referred to as alley or corridor stage.

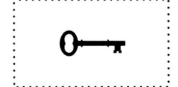

Found space
A theatre space in which the architecture is an essential element of the performance, or a non-theatre space that is temporarily transformed into a performance venue.

Existing performance spaces
- Research each of the performance spaces listed above to find:

  ☑ photographs of existing spaces.
  ☑ ground plans of each of the spaces.
  ☑ photographs of productions that take place in each of these types of spaces.

- Create a collage for each performance space and add your own notes regarding what sort of theatre you might stage in each of these spaces.

Choosing your performance space

When choosing a performance space for your theatre work (be it a theoretical production or an actual piece you plan to stage), you should always begin by thinking about the specific piece of theatre you are creating, where it will be set, what the piece is about and the sort of experience you want the audience to have.

Alongside these artistic considerations you will also need to think about the following.

Audience
- Audience size
- Where the audience will be positioned (close, above, below, or far away from the action)
- Audience sightlines (the audience's view of the action)
- The acoustics of the space
- How the audience will experience the action (intimate, as witnesses, immersed, detached and so on.)

Performers
- How much space the performers have to move
- Where the performers will enter or exit (e.g. if there are wings or if entrance is through audience)
- Proxemics — where and how performers are positioned in the action and their relationship to each other, to the audience, the space and anything else that is in the space
- Use of body and voice in the space
- Use of what is in the space
- Use of levels

Further research
Research the area of proxemics and think about how this will inform your approach to theatre-making.

Design
- The type of set used (e.g. in theatre in-the-round, the set is usually below the eye level of the audience so that sightlines are not restricted)
- Use of levels to raise or lower some of the action and to create different locations and focal points
- The positioning of the set and props (e.g. backdrop, individual set pieces)
- The positioning of lights and the lighting control desk
- The positioning of sound and the sound control desk
- The amount of detail needed in costume, set, props (this will vary depending on how close the audience is to the action)

The following activities are designed to engage you with the dynamics of performance spaces and to equip you with an understanding of different spaces, their possibilities and their limitations.

Activity

The positioning of the audience
- Take two chairs and position them facing each other (any distance apart). Photograph this and imagine this is the set at the beginning of a scene. Turn one chair upside down and position it elsewhere in the space. Photograph this and think of it as the end of the scene.
- Create three moments of dramatic action that lead the stage action or narrative from the opening position of the chairs to the final position. The falling and movement of the chair must happen within the scene as part of the action.
- Photograph each of the three moments of action that take us from the first photograph to the last. Arrange the photographs in sequence and add any text/captions for each photograph to capture any dialogue that is spoken in the scene. This sequence of photographs will now be your "performance material".
- Once you have rehearsed your scene, take 10 chairs that are going to represent the audience. Now re-direct the scene so it can be performed to the following audience formations.

  ☑ With the chairs in a circle to create an in-the-round performance space
  ☑ With the chairs in two lines facing each other and at a distance from each other to create a traverse performance space
  ☑ With the chairs in a line facing the space to create an end-on performance space
  ☑ In a found, non-performance space somewhere in the school that will accommodate 10 chairs

- Present your scenes in the different places and reflect on the significance of the performance space and shape. Discuss and record what effect you think the performance space has on:

  ☑ the audience experience
  ☑ the director's and designer's shaping of the space.

A space of significance
It is helpful to think of a performance space as an empty space that commands an audience's attention. Everything that is put in the space or that happens in the space signals meaning to the audience. In this respect it becomes significant because everything in the space becomes a sign that is interpreted by the audience. This is as true of performance elements (e.g. a gesture, a word, a movement) as it is of production elements (e.g. a lighting state, a prop, a piece of scenery).

You can think of these theatrical signs as having three different purposes.

1. They have a **function**. For example, when someone exits and someone calls after them, the performer is required to raise their voice to be heard or a chair is needed on stage because the character has to sit.

2. They provide us with **information**. For example, the way a character speaks or moves tells us what historical period the play is set in or the style of the chair tells us if the household is wealthy or poor.

3. They act as **symbols**, communicating some sort of idea to the audience. For example, a handshake between two people who have been enemies signifies peace and harmony or a throne raised on a platform signifies royalty or power.

Activity

Making *significance*
- Choose one of the following objects.

  - ☑ A children's toy
  - ☑ A piece of rope
  - ☑ A cup

- Create three short theatrical moments, showing the object as **functional**, as **informative**, and as **symbolic**.
- Choose one of the following actions.

  - ☑ Turning your back on someone
  - ☑ Kneeling
  - ☑ Waving

- Create three short theatrical moments, showing the action as **functional**, as **informative**, as **symbolic**.
- Discuss how you used the objects and actions and how each different moment changed their significance.

Further research
Research the semiotics of theatre and how creators, designers, directors and performers use signs to communicate with the audience

The use of performance and production elements
A performance space is never static. It is constantly changing and shifting. A performance space is changed through the use of the following elements.

- **Performance elements**
  How performers use their body and voice, their positioning in the space (blocking).

- **Production elements**
  The use of scenic and technical elements such as lighting, sound, projection, special effects, costumes, props, use of levels, and so on.

Activity

The performer and the space
- Using some chairs to mark the area, create a theatre in-the-round performance space.
- In the space position a bag, a coat and one piece of furniture.
- With you or your partner taking on the role of performer, carry out the following actions.

  - ☑ The performer enters the space
  - ☑ The performer interacts with one or more of the objects
  - ☑ The performer says the line "Now I understand". This can be said at any point in the scene.

- Think about how the shape of the performance space affected the action.
- Recreate and re-enact the scene for the following scenarios.

  - ☑ For a proscenium performance space
  - ☑ For a thrust performance space
  - ☑ To make the audience feel sympathy for the character
  - ☑ To make the audience dislike the character

- Think about how the performer changes the nature of the space and how the space changes both the meaning and the experience of the audience. Discuss your thoughts with your partner.

Activity

Changing places using production elements

- Working in pairs or small groups. The following activity can be undertaken either through discussion or through practical work. Mark out a large circle or square on the floor. This will be your performance space. Decide how you would use performance and production elements to suggest a transformation in the space from one location to another for each of the following.

  ☑ A modern city square transforms into an ancient, peaceful temple
  ☑ A war bunker transforms into a deserted beach
  ☑ An attic room transforms into a shopping mall
  ☑ An underground tunnel transforms into the top of a fairy-tale tower

- Make notes on how you proposed using production elements to signify location and to change from one location to another.
- Present your ideas to the class through demonstration or through discussion using visual materials.

2.4 Staging: Performance elements

Performance elements are defined by the *Theatre guide* as the performer's use of **body** (such as face, gesture, posture, body language or manipulation of objects), **voice** (such as pitch, pace, pause, tone, volume, emphasis or intonation) and the placement and movement of performers on the stage.

All students are required to perform in the theatre course. This includes performing live for an audience, presenting your explorations of a performance convention to camera and also performing in collaboration with others as part of an ensemble. You also need to be able to consider as director-designers how performance elements can be employed to bring a play text to life and to create moments of tension, emotion, atmosphere and/or meaning for an audience.

The development of your performance skills and understanding how to use them, therefore, is an important part of the theatre course.

One of the best ways to develop your performance skills is through practical work and through activities that engage your body and voice. Training for the development of performance skills can generally be categorized as exercises that focus on the following.

- Control and use of body
- Movement skills
- Vocal work
- Breathing
- Relaxation
- Body awareness
- Characterization
- Energizing

- Contact work
- Use of emotions
- Rhythm
- Focus and concentration
- Use of space
- Working with others
- Eye contact
- Being present and centered

Further research
There are different philosophies and ideas regarding performance training as well as different approaches. Research performance training to discover what some practitioners and theorists believe is the best approach to training. You might also want to look at some higher education settings (such as drama colleges, universities, training centres) and see what their approaches are.

It is important to frame your work as a performer in relation to the effect your performance will have on an audience, as well as how to elicit a particular response from the audience.

Activity

Developing performance skills

- Choose three of the performance training areas from the list on the previous page. These may be areas that you feel you need to develop further or areas that are new to you.
- Research and find three exercises for each of the chosen areas that you can experiment with on your own.
- Run through these exercises and film yourself experimenting with them over a period of time. Review the clips and think about how the exercises might help develop your skills.
- Make notes on how you think a performer changes the nature of a performance space and how the space changes both the meaning and the experience of the audience.
- Discuss your thoughts with a partner.

Activity

Preparing the body and voice for performance

- It is important with any activity—be it performance, sport, or fitness—that uses the body and/or voice as its main tool, that the body and/or voice is fully prepared before use. This is what we call the warm-up. With this in mind, create a 15-minute warm-up that you can easily do before any performance or performance training. The warm-up should include both physical and vocal activities.
- Exchange warm-up ideas with a partner or lead a group through the stages of your warm-up.

Performance style

In all theatre-making work, it is important for you to be aware of different styles of performance. Performance style can be determined by some or all of the following.

- The material you are working with
- The style of a play text
- The historical period
- The setting
- What is considered culturally appropriate
- A theatre tradition
- A theatre theorist
- A social or political movement

Performance style also plays a major part in creating the world of a play on stage and communicating this world to an audience. It is therefore closely related to what you, as a theatre-maker, want your audience to experience, the effect you want the piece to have on them and what information you want them to have about the created world.

The performance style often influences a performer in the following ways.

- How they use their body and/or voice
- How they interact with the audience
- How they interact with other performers
- How they use the performance space
- How they employ or respond to production elements (such as set, costume, props, lights, sound.)

Activity

Performance style scribbles
- Research and write a list of performance styles.
- Choose five of these styles to focus on and carry out further research into them. What are the key elements? How are they distinguished?
- On a large sheet of paper, write a series of key words that you think go with each style.
- Draw pictures, patterns or scribbles that you think gives a sense of the performance style, to accompany your chosen words.
- Photograph this page for your journal.

Activity

Different worlds, different performance styles
- Working with a partner or in a small group, choose one of the lines of text from the list below that describe different worlds.

  ➤ "It was a world of cogs and wheels, a world of industry, the factory and the mine, where chimneys spewed smoke into the air and no one saw the light of day. Here we lived."

  ➤ "It was a world of thirst and hunger, where under the burning sun nothing would yield its produce, where the rivers ran dry and the earth cried out for water. Here we lived."

  ➤ "It was a world of coming and going, of flight and escape, arrivals and departures, a place of exile, of checkpoints and borders, of searching and searching and never belonging. Here we lived."

  ➤ "It was a world of longing, of wishing and dreaming, of watching the blossom drifting on the breeze, of listening to the water flowing along the stream and wondering what and if and whether. Here we lived."

- Think about how to best use your voice—what style you're going to choose—to read this text in order to give the listener a feeling of this world. For example, will it be realistic, exaggerated, stylized?
- With this in mind, capture an audio recording of the text being read out loud.
- Consider what movement(s) might accompany the audio recording to add another dimension to this created world and to help an audience perceive it more powerfully. Experiment with practising the movements alongside the audio recording.
- Perform this to another pair or small group and discuss the choices that were most effective and why.

Performance style and the audience

Different performance styles can have different effects on an audience and can achieve different theatrical intentions. As such, choosing a performance style for your work will depend on what you want the audience to experience.

Realism and naturalism, for example, are performance styles that are often used if you want an audience to be emotionally moved by the theatre piece or if you want the action to be more believable. Epic theatre is a performance style that is often used for political plays or to make an audience think. When creating original theatre you have freedom to choose the performance style(s) of the piece of theatre and you may even decide to use a variety of performance styles, depending on what you want your piece to achieve.

Top tip
Performance style is a key artistic choice when it comes to any performance and should be something that you think about and make a decision on.

If you are working with a play text, the performance style might be dictated by the historical period, cultural setting and location in which the play takes place. In some instances, you might decide, depending on your interpretation of a play text, that you wish to present it in a style other than the one that naturally fits it. If you choose to alter the style, make sure you have a strong rationale for this. Shakespeare is a playwright whose plays are very often directed and staged in historical periods, cultures and places different to the ones indicated by the text and this inevitably leads to Shakespearean plays being regularly performed using a diverse range of performance styles.

Capturing your skills development

Video recording individual and group performances offers you the opportunity to watch yourself and your group, to evaluate your own work and to examine how your performance skills are developing.

It is helpful to get used to setting a camera device to regularly capture your performance work in progress. These recordings can form an invaluable part of your theatre journal. They can also be used to create a specific performance skills video journal that captures the development of your skills over the duration of the course alongside your other ongoing reflections and evaluations.

2.5 Staging: Production elements

Production elements are defined in the *Theatre guide* as **scenic** elements (such as the design of the space, set, props, costume) and **technical** elements (such as the design of lighting, sound, multimedia and/or special effects). You should think of the individual elements as "tools of the theatre experience", with each tool being purposefully deployed in order to craft and shape moments of theatre and to have an effect on the audience.

Production elements play an important part in creating the world of a piece of theatre—its mood, atmosphere and where it is located. Regardless of whether the piece of theatre is set in the real world or taking place in some sort of abstract cosmos, the production elements provide an audience with a wealth of information, as well as being a key factor in determining how the audience experiences the piece.

It is useful to think about production elements in the following ways.

- As informative—giving information regarding time and place; where we are and when we are there
- As evocative—evoking emotions and communicating ideas
- As sensory—engaging the senses and creating an atmosphere
- As functional—having a particular practical purpose, such as costume to dress the performer or lighting to focus the audience on specific moments of action

In this respect, it is important that you develop your production skills by engaging with production elements practically so that you understand the following areas.

- Functionality—what each production element is capable of doing
- Design—the artistic choices you make regarding how the production elements will be used individually and in combination with each other
- Effect—the effect each production element has on both the audience and the performers
- Application and operation—the use, operation and application of these elements to stage action (for example, knowing how to use sound equipment)

Production elements in our world

- Choose two spaces that you are familiar with and can access easily. One should be an **interior** and the other an **exterior** (for example, the kitchen in a house, a public park).
- Take yourself to each of these spaces. For five minutes, observe the spaces closely and write notes in the table below to capture how each of the spaces could feasibly be re-created on stage.

Activity

Set	Lighting	Costume	Sound
• What shapes do you see in the space? What objects, furniture or structures are most visible? • Sketch a small plan of the location in the space below and mark the key features. • Mark where you think the focal point of the space is with an X.	• Where are the light sources in this space? Mark these on the plan you have drawn. • What colours do you see at this time of day? Add these to the plan and shade any dark areas or shadow. Mark any spaces that are particularly well lit with an asterisk.	• What do you see people in the space wearing? • Which specific items of clothing do you associate with this place? • Sketch a rough drawing of a person in the space to indicate their clothing and to show how the clothes are shaped by their body.	• Write a list of everything you can hear that you think contributes to the atmosphere. • Capture a short audio recording of the sound in the space. Listen to the recording and describe the atmosphere the sounds create.

Set and lighting		Costume	Sound
Interior location			

Set and lighting		Costume	Sound
Exterior location			

Principles of design

Some of the key production elements are presented below along with some of the key principles regarding their use and their design. It is helpful to become familiar with these as you begin to develop your own pieces of theatre or to inspire ideas for hypothetical productions.

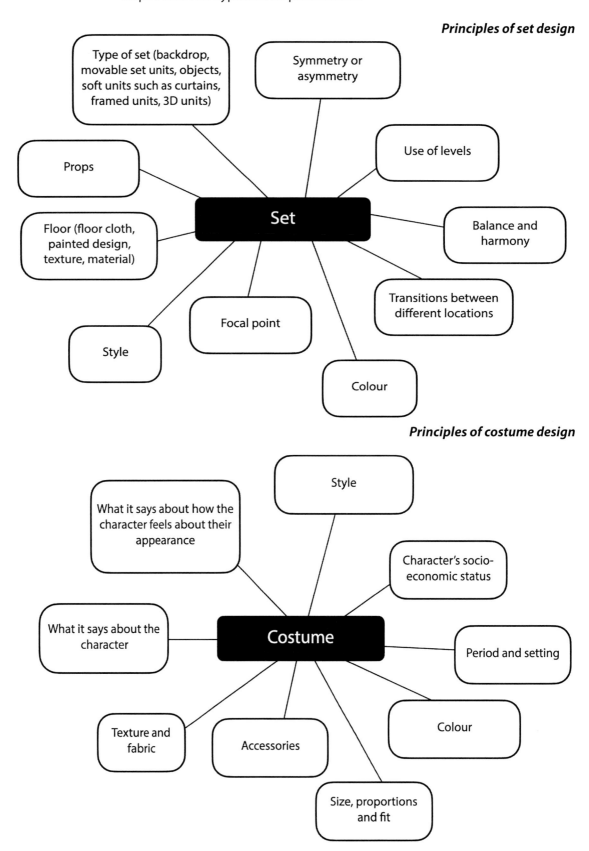

Principles of set design

Type of set (backdrop, movable set units, objects, soft units such as curtains, framed units, 3D units)

Symmetry or asymmetry

Use of levels

Props

Set

Balance and harmony

Floor (floor cloth, painted design, texture, material)

Transitions between different locations

Style

Focal point

Colour

Principles of costume design

Style

What it says about how the character feels about their appearance

Character's socio-economic status

What it says about the character

Costume

Period and setting

Texture and fabric

Accessories

Colour

Size, proportions and fit

Principles of lighting design

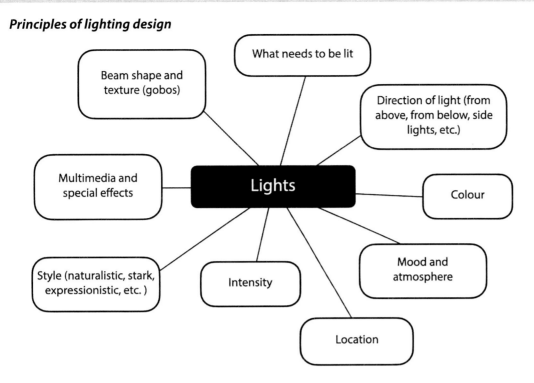

Principles of sound design

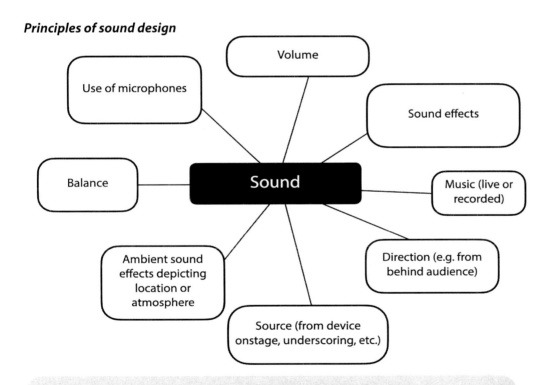

Production elements in productions you have experienced
- Think of a production that you have experienced as an audience member or watch a recorded theatre production online.
- Choose a scene or a moment from the production where the set, costume, lighting and sound effects made an impression on you because they were used in a way that was effective or unusual.
- Using the principles of design illustrated above, discuss how each of the production elements were used individually and in relationship with each other to create a powerful effect.

Activity

Experimenting with production elements

The best way to learn about production elements is to play with them and to experiment. A fully equipped theatre space is not required for you to do this, although if one is available, then of course make full use of it! The following resources can be used as a way of exploring each production element.

Set

- Any physical objects or pieces that can be put together as a set to transform the space (such as furniture, fabric, flats, rugs)

Costume

- Any items of clothing or materials that can be used to dress the body or alter the face (such as fabric, old clothes, shoes, hats, glasses, accessories, paper, masks, red noses, make-up)

Props

- Any objects that have resonance and that can be used for multifunctional purposes (such as rope, household objects, newspapers, books, umbrellas, sticks, brooms, telephones, puppets, toys, photographs)

Lighting

- Anything that can create light and shadow and that can be used to light up both a space and performer(s) (such as flashlights, candles, phones, desk lamps, household lamps with naked bulbs, fabric to blackout windows)

Sound

- Anything that can play music or sounds (such as a laptop, tablet, phone, wired microphone, speaker) and anything that creates sound effects (such as pre-recorded tracks, your own voice, digital soundscapes created through apps, instruments)

Projection and multimedia

- Anything that can be projected or that can play images or film (such as TV, handheld devices, projector)

Playing with production elements
- Either create the following with whatever you can find or design them using images/drawings/audio.

  - ☑ A place of isolation using lights and sound
  - ☑ A celebration using sound and props
  - ☑ An old-fashioned, haunted children's room using set and lights
  - ☑ A hospital room using costume and sound
  - ☑ A clearing in the forest using set, lights and sound
  - ☑ A city street using projection and props
  - ☑ A tense meeting at home using lights and sound
  - ☑ A children's play area using costume and props

- Now see if you can create each of those choosing only **one** of the following:

  - ☑ Light
  - ☑ Sound
  - ☑ Object
  - ☑ Piece of furniture
  - ☑ Costume

2.6 Theatre-maker intentions and responsible theatre-making

Theatre is a form of communication, an interaction between theatre-maker and audience. It is an event when you have an audience's attention for a fixed period of time so you can share your thoughts, perspectives and feelings about the world.

Theatre-maker intentions are your plans for what you want to do in that time, why you want to do it, the experience an audience will have and how you will achieve it.

Working with clearly defined theatre-maker intentions also encourages responsible theatre-making by requiring you to consider the purpose of what you are presenting to an audience and what you want them to experience.

Theatre-maker intentions serve a practical purpose, providing you with:

- **purpose**—a clear goal and rationale for what you want to make and why you want to make it
- **guidance**—something you can refer to that guides the development of your work and keeps you on track, reminding you of what you set out to do
- **a measure**—something you can use to evaluate the extent to which you have been successful, helping you to decide what to change, develop or discard.

Activity

Reflecting on intention
- Reflect on what you personally think is the purpose of theatre. What function does it have in a community? What would the world be like without it? Complete the following sentence:

  "For me, theatre's main purpose is to..."

- Close your eyes. Imagine you have no restrictions and no budget. What type of theatre would you like to make? What would it look like? Complete the following sentence.

  "The sort of theatre I would like to make is ..."

- How would you like your theatre to affect the audience? Why would you want to do this? How would you do it? Complete the following sentence.

  "I want the theatre I make to ... because ..."

- Write down your completed sentences and share them with a partner.

Theatre-maker intentions and the theatre assessment tasks
Theatre-maker intentions are a key feature of all the theatre syllabus areas, but you are also required to formulate theatre-maker intentions in three of the four assessment tasks. These are the production proposal, the collaborative project and the HL solo theatre piece.

Though theatre-maker intentions are defined slightly differently depending on the context and content of the assessment task, they do have some common ingredients.

Developing theatre-maker intentions

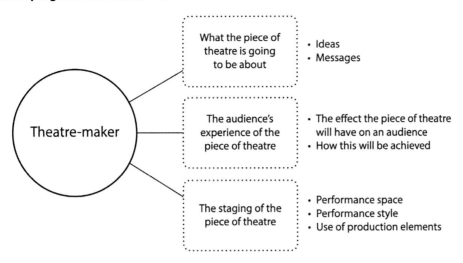

The diagram above illustrates how the theatre assessment tasks require you to articulate your theatre-maker intentions. The task below asks you to consider how each assessment task requires you to work in different ways.

Theatre-maker intentions by task
- Look at the different theatre-maker intentions definitions below and overleaf for each each assessment task, taken from the guide.
- What are the similarities and differences in each task? What does each need to include? Write notes on each task in these spaces provided.

Activity

PRODUCTION PROPOSAL

Definition of theatre-maker intentions for this task

- Students are required to identify specific intentions for their work. Theatre-maker intentions refer to the student's interpretation of what they consider to be the key ideas of the play, their decisions regarding how they will stage this interpretation and what effect they intend this to have on an audience.
- Within their intentions, students must also identify their choice of performance style (for example, naturalistic, surreal, and so on) and their choice of performance space for the proposed staging.

Required aspects of theatre-maker intentions

COLLABORATIVE PROJECT

Definition of theatre-maker intentions for this task

- Students are required to collaboratively formulate intentions for the piece of theatre (200 words maximum). These must be agreed by the ensemble and should include the following.

  ☑ The chosen starting point
  ☑ What the piece will address or explore
  ☑ The target audience for the piece
  ☑ The performance space and the positioning of the audience
  ☑ The effect the ensemble aims to have on their target audience

Required aspects of theatre-maker intentions

SOLO THEATRE PIECE (HL ONLY)

Definition of theatre-maker intentions for this task

- Early on in the process students are required to formulate theatre-maker intentions for the solo performance. These defined intentions should clearly articulate what will be performed and the effect that the student intends their piece to have on an audience. Each student's theatre-maker intentions should be aligned with the following.

  ☑ The theatre theorist's overarching intentions (which may be theatrical, social, political, philosophical and so on)
  ☑ The purpose of these intentions regarding the effect the theorist wishes their theatre to have on the audience

Required aspects of theatre-maker intentions

It is important to recognize that intention is not just something abstract, but rather something which determines all of the artistic choices in the creation of theatre and the eventual experience for the audience. Decisions around performance style, design and the use of production elements are all guided by the theatre-maker intentions.

Choosing an audience

Being aware of who the audience might be or choosing which audience you want is an important part both in formulating theatre-maker intentions and determining the nature of the theatre experience the audience will have.

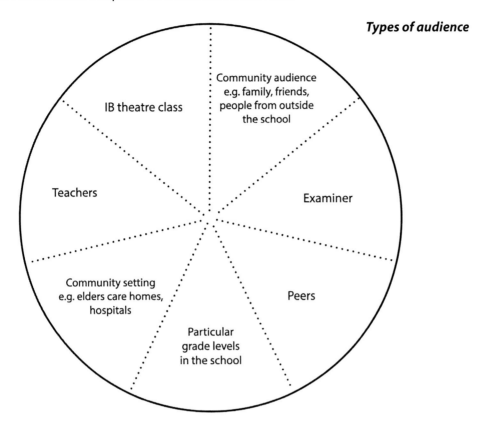

Types of audience

In a school context the audience will sometimes be decided by what is feasible for the context of your school, so check with your teacher when specifying an audience.

Creating and presenting theatre, as well as understanding what's needed to make theatre, is a requirement of the course and some of the assessment tasks. It is important, therefore, that you have experience of preparing work for actual audiences and of presenting to these audiences.

Audience and theatre-maker intentions
- Imagine you are going to create a piece of theatre about injustice. Write a theatre-maker intention using some of the information from earlier in this chapter regarding what you should include in the creation of your intention.
- Now rewrite that intention for an audience of:

  ☑ 7-year-olds
  ☑ people over the age of 14
  ☑ people who have experienced injustice
  ☑ families (possibly with young children) in the audience
  ☑ political leaders attending a conference on combating injustice.

- Discuss with a partner the extent to which knowing a specific target audience can affect theatre-maker intentions and the style of the developing theatre piece.

Activity

As well as choosing an audience in the theatre course, you are also required to capture audience feedback for both the collaborative project and the HL solo theatre piece assessment tasks. You will be expected to evaluate the extent to which your theatre-maker intentions for each piece have been met. As such, the nature and make-up of your chosen audience needs to be determined from the start of the process. You will need to keep your audience in mind while you create your pieces in order to ensure that your work fulfils your intended effects.

2.7 Moments of tension, emotion, atmosphere and/or meaning

Theatre is a live art form that takes place in real time. In that respect, it is an uninterrupted experience, except for any sort of scheduled intervals or planned interruptions. You may find it useful to consider theatre in this course as a series of specially constructed and crafted moments, with one moment purposefully connected to the other. With this in mind, you could think of the overall audience experience as being made up of an accumulation of moments, carefully constructed by the theatre-maker with full consideration of individual performance and production elements as well as how these work together to create a particular effect on the audience.

The theatre course provides a useful framework for the construction of such experiences by classifying theatrical moments into four categories: moments of tension; moments of emotion; moments of atmosphere; and/or moments of meaning. These are collectively known by the acronym "TEAM".

Moments of "TEAM" do not have any particular minimum or maximum time limit associated with them. They are focused moments which contain pieces of action (either with text or without text) that have one or more of the "TEAM" attributes.

Moments of tension
- These are the moments within a piece of theatre where the performer(s) finds themselves in a tense situation. For example, facing an obstacle, being in conflict, in a state of anticipation, negotiating internal or external struggles. Tension is often seen as the heart of dramatic action. Moments of tension are also moments when an audience feels tense, either because they are experiencing the action in the same way as the performer(s) or because, as an audience, they have more information than a character within the piece has. For example, the person a character is talking to is holding a knife, there is a searchlight moving towards them, we know that they are the cause of a disaster, or perhaps their secret is about to be revealed. This is the cause of a heightened audience sensation of tension commonly known as suspense.

Moments of emotion
- These are moments within a piece of theatre that either depict or communicate the emotion of the character(s) on stage or that evoke an emotional response from the audience. This could be any of a wide range of emotions from deep despair to complete jubilation. This might be an emotion arising out of a situation, a character's inner turmoil, or from a movement sequence that manages to capture an emotion that we cannot quite put into words. In some instances, of course, the emotion depicted on stage might, in fact, evoke a contrasting emotional response from the audience, the classic example being the laugh that erupts when seeing someone slip on a banana skin.

Moments of atmosphere
- A precise definition of what constitutes atmosphere in a piece of theatre is difficult because it is about something that is evocative, sensory and that we often cannot put our finger on. It evokes particular sensual and emotional responses within us. It is what is commonly used to position us within the context of a particular setting, be that a location (the woods on a summer's day, a graveyard at night) or an emotional situation (the return of a soldier from war, the death of a character). Atmosphere is often created by the aesthetics of stage action. It can be created by a variety of theatrical devices, from rain falling on stage, mist rising from a grate, the sound of a heartbeat, a group of performers walking slowly across the space or a piece of music quietly underscoring spoken words.

Moments of meaning
- Every moment in a piece of theatre could arguably be considered a moment of meaning insofar as every moment in a piece of theatre is communicating something to the audience. The most useful way to think about moments of meaning is to consider them as moments that are primarily concerned with relaying and communicating the key themes, ideas, messages and concepts that the maker(s) of the piece of theatre wish to communicate and to engage the audience with.

You need to understand the make-up of these moments and how to effectively craft them using performance and production elements. The following activities introduce you to moments of "TEAM", exploring how they can be constructed and how they can be identified.

Moments
- Working in pairs or in a small group, create the following moments for an audience.

    - ☑ The moment a secret is revealed
    - ☑ The moment good news arrives
    - ☑ The moment when everything changes
    - ☑ The moment when you discover a place is haunted
    - ☑ The moment when you realize you are powerless

- Once you have experimented with each moment, decide whether each of these situations would be considered as a moment of tension, emotion, atmosphere or meaning. What are the elements that define it? What would you have to do to change what sort of moment it is?
- Choose one of these moments and create a new scene that takes place before the moment. This is the lead in to the moment. Next, create the scene that takes place after the moment.
- Discuss the various lengths that a moment on stage can take. Make a clear decision about how long your chosen moment will take, and do not feel you have to prolong the time it takes.
- Show this sequence of scenes (before the moment, the moment, and following the moment) to others and discuss to what extent the effect of the moment is determined by what goes before and what comes after.

Making moments in theatre using performance and production elements

- Working in pairs, choose one performance element and one production element from the following.

  ➤ *Performance elements*
  - ☑ Use of body
  - ☑ Use of voice
  - ☑ Use of space

  ➤ *Production elements*
  - ☑ Use of set
  - ☑ Use of costume
  - ☑ Use of lights
  - ☑ Use of sound

- Using the single performance element and production element you have chosen, create a moment of tension, emotion, atmosphere or meaning based on the theme of "acceptance".
- Show your moment and discuss with others how you used the performance and production element individually and how you used them together to create the type of moment you selected. What made it effective?

The next activity asks you to identify the various ingredients that create the various attributes of the moments of "TEAM". This is not a definitive list, but there are some basic ingredients that are useful for you to think about. For example, contrast is one of the common ingredients in the creation of tension, moving from quiet to loud, from light to dark, from fast to slow, and so on.

Understanding moments of "TEAM"

- Working individually, in pairs or in a small group, choose one of the following prompts.

  - ☑ **Tension:** the moment before a fight breaks out
  - ☑ **Emotion:** the moment when someone leaves home
  - ☑ **Atmosphere:** the atmosphere of a hospital waiting room
  - ☑ **Meaning:** a moment that communicates acceptance of a situation or given circumstance

- Without using any dialogue or by limiting dialogue to no more than five spoken lines maximum, create a scene that illustrates the chosen prompt.
- Present your scene to others and ask your audience to identify how tension, emotion, atmosphere or meaning were created in your scene. If you are working alone, film your scene and review it to identify the ingredients.
- List the ingredients that helped to create the moment of tension, emotion, atmosphere or meaning in the table opposite.

Which element of "TEAM" did you choose to create?

What do you think makes this element of "TEAM"?

How might you show this element of "TEAM" on stage?

What causes tension/emotion/atmosphere/meaning in the moment you have worked on?

How else could tension/emotion/atmosphere/meaning be created?

Activity

Identifying moments of "TEAM" in a play text

- Read through the script extract below and identify possible moments of "TEAM" in the scene. Remember that a moment does not have any maximum time or minimum time limit. It can be a moment with dialogue or a moment of action.
- Working with a partner or in a small group, stage one of the moments you have identified. Decide on the performance space and how you will use performance elements to create the intended effect.
- Discuss how you identified features of moments of "TEAM" in the text and how these were then transformed into action using performance elements.
- Now consider how production elements could be used in the chosen moment to enhance it further. What set, costume, lights, sound, effects might you use?

SCRIPT EXTRACT: *Macbeth* by William Shakespeare

ACT I - SCENE I. A deserted place.

Thunder and lightning. Enter three Witches

First Witch:	When shall we three meet again?
	In thunder, lightning, or in rain?
Second Witch:	When the hurlyburly's done,
	When the battle's lost and won.
Third Witch:	That will be ere the set of sun.
First Witch:	Where the place?
Second Witch:	Upon the heath.
Third Witch:	There to meet with Macbeth.
First Witch:	I come, Graymalkin!
Second Witch:	Paddock calls.
Third Witch:	Anon.
ALL:	Fair is foul, and foul is fair:
	Hover through the fog and filthy air.

Exeunt

SCENE II. A camp near Forres.

Alarum within. Enter DUNCAN, MALCOLM, DONALBAIN, LENNOX, with Attendants, meeting a bleeding Sergeant

DUNCAN:	What bloody man is that? He can report,
	As seemeth by his plight, of the revolt
	The newest state.
MALCOLM:	This is the sergeant
	Who like a good and hardy soldier fought
	'Gainst my captivity. Hail, brave friend!
	Say to the king the knowledge of the broil
	As thou didst leave it.

Further research
Choose your own play text and read through the opening. Does the play begin a moment of "TEAM"? What makes you think that? How might you use some of the techniques explored in this chapter to enhance this moment of "TEAM" for the audience?

Chapter 2: Recap

In this chapter we have explored the fundamentals of the IB Diploma Programme theatre course, focusing on:

- the four stages of the theatre-making process and how this applies to your work and the assessment tasks

- the four theatre-maker perspectives that focus on artistic approaches to your work and identify the skills you need to develop

- the performance space and how this effects both the performance and the experience of the audience

- how you can develop your performance skills and how performance elements can be used

- production elements and how these can be used to create an experience for the audience and communicate the ideas of a performance piece

- the importance of theatre-maker intentions and how these can be used to guide your work and clarify your purpose

- how theatre is made up of moments of tension, emotion, atmosphere and/or meaning and how these can be recognized and constructed using performance and production elements.

3. Staging play texts and the production proposal

You can either work individually, in pairs or in small groups for all of the activities in this chapter.

Introduction

This chapter addresses the following areas of staging play texts.

3.1   Productions you have experienced
3.2   Choosing a play text
3.3   The ideas in the play text
3.4   Theatre-maker intentions
3.5   Visual design ideas
3.6   Staging moments of tension, emotion, atmosphere and/or meaning
3.7   Preparing for assessment: Structuring your production proposal

The staging play texts syllabus area engages you with play texts and the processes involved in transforming a play text into stage action using performance and production elements. It requires you to explain, using words and visuals, how you imagine this play will be turned from a text into an audience experience. This area is assessed through the production proposal task.

Why is this area important?

A play text is something that has been written to be performed. It requires the theatre-maker to imagine what it would be like in performance as they read it. You are, in effect, translating the words you read into action. In your mind's eye you are seeing people, dressed and acting in a particular way, in some sort of setting that has a particular kind of atmosphere. You are also hearing, in your head, the words spoken by the characters in a particular way and there may also be other sounds or music that give a sense of the location or create a particular type of feeling. In other words, you are translating the play into an experience for an audience—an experience that they are going to access through their senses.

Proposing your own production

The production proposal assessment task requires you to think like a theatre director and like a designer. Understanding how these artists use their skills to bring a text to life is therefore a key part of this process. The best way to learn about directing and designing theatre is to take every opportunity during your course to actually direct and design, even if it is only for short scenes or excepts from play texts. Reading a variety of play texts, written in different styles and from different periods and cultures, will also give you the chance to begin to see what plays most interest you.

What the guide says

For the production proposal assessment task each student in the ensemble is required to submit the following.

- A production proposal (a maximum of 12 pages of written text and images) plus a list of all sources used.
- The written text must not exceed 4,000 words.
- The list of any sources used is excluded from the page count.
- The production proposal is assessed on screen. You must ensure that the work is clear and legible when presented in a digital, on-screen format. The work should be created using a common page size (A4 or US Letter), be typed in a legible sans serif 12-point font and use standard margin sizes and single spacing. The production proposal may also contain legible handwriting.

Definition: Production proposal

A production proposal communicates your vision for the staging of a play text for an audience. It is a hypothetical proposal (so it doesn't actually happen) but it does need to be *feasible* – meaning that your ideas and suggestions could realistically be possible to stage in real life. Your proposal should persuasively explain how performance and production elements could potentially work on stage to fulfil your theatre-maker intentions.

To achieve this, the production proposal task requires you to undertake the following process.

- Choose your own play text.
- Identify the ideas in the play text.
- Consider the effect you would want your production to have on an audience
- Formulate theatre-maker intentions for how you would stage the play text, using performance and production elements to transform it into an experience for the audience.
- Imagine the performance space, visualize the action that takes place in this space and propose creative design ideas regarding costume, lights, set, props, sound, and so on.
- Imagine how you would stage a moment of tension, emotion, atmosphere and/ or meaning ("TEAM") that you have identified in the play text, explaining how performance and production elements would create this moment so it achieves its impact.

The production proposal assessment task does not require you to actually stage the play. This is a proposal explaining how you would **theoretically** go about staging it and reasons for your choices. You can, of course, try ideas out, experimenting with yourself and others to bring the text to life so you can check if these ideas work.

Freeing your creative imagination

A play text, like an architectural plan, needs to be interpreted and transformed into stage action in the same way that an architectural plan needs to be transformed into a building. This task really allows you to be truly imaginative. Your vision for the staging of the play text is not restrained by considering your own school setting or budgets. You can literally stage the play anywhere you want, using any resources, as long as this is justified and feasible—performing a play on the moon is not as yet a feasible option!

Assessment criteria

The production proposal is assessed using the following criteria.

	Production proposal	Marks	Total
A	Ideas and intentions	8	
B	The proposed design	4	20
C	The proposed staging of one moment of the play	8	

The activities outlined in this chapter have been designed to fully prepare you for success in each of these areas.

3.1 Productions you have experienced

Experiencing professional productions, either live or digitally, is one of the best ways to develop your directing/designing skills. Productions of play texts will show you how written words have been transformed into an experience for the audience by a team of professionals through the use of performance and production skills.

Reflecting on a past theatre experience
- Think about a production that you have experienced as an audience member and that was significant to you. Using the spaces provided, write your reflections in response to each of the prompts given.

Activity

Reflection on a significant production

Title of the production

Date of the production

Why do you think this experience has stayed with you?

Describe one specific moment from the production that you thought was effective.
Describe what the performer(s) were doing and what production skills were used.

Explain why you think this moment was so effective.

Draw a picture of this moment. You can do it with stick figures. Mark the space and where the audience was seated.

What do you think was the intention for staging this piece? What did the production hope to achieve? Did it have a message? What experience do you think the director and designer wanted the audience to have and why?

3.2 Choosing a play text

This section provides some guidance to help you choose a play text for this task. It can be used when choosing plays to experiment with in preparation for the task or for the actual assessment task itself.

What to look for when choosing a play text

A play text that you are interested in and that you would like to bring to life
You should choose a play text that excites you and that you would like to stage. You might also want to think why this play text is relevant to an audience at this moment in time. It should be a play text that gets you thinking and that you can visualize on stage. It should be one that you think you can do exciting and creative things with.

A play text that deals with several interesting ideas
The play text should deal with ideas, themes or issues. Play texts say something about life, people and the world. The creators of play texts are often trying to communicate their point of view. These points of view can either capture something we already know but which we could not put into words ourselves or give us new understandings and insights into worlds that are not familiar to us. Play texts can entertain us but they can also teach us.

A play text that has creative possibilities for performers
As a director you need to have an idea of how the play text will be brought to life by the performers. You need to choose a play text that gives performers opportunities to be creative and that gives you, as the director, the chance to be imaginative with performers. Think about the style of performance—for example, will it be realistic, symbolic, movement-based?

A play text that has exciting possibilities for design and for the use of production elements
You should also approach choosing a play text from a design point of view. This involves visualizing the play and thinking about what sort of space it might be performed in and what set, lights, costumes, sound, props and/or special effects you might use to bring it to life.

A play text that has interesting moments of action
When you read the play text you should be able to identify key moments of action that you think would be exciting to stage. You should be able to visualize how these moments can be staged to have maximum impact on an audience.

Once you have read your chosen play, you are ready to complete the following exercises.

My chosen play text

- Capture your reasons for selecting the play you have chosen using the space below.

What interests me about this play?

Why is this play text interesting to me?	
How can this play text be relevant to an audience?	
What are some of the key ideas in the play text?	
What are some of the creative opportunities for performers?	
What are some of the creative opportunities for design and for the use of production elements?	
What might be some key moments of action in the play text?	

3.3 The ideas in the play text

When you read a play, you are partly being a detective, searching for clues that will unlock its meaning. The ideas that the playwright has chosen to focus on make up this meaning. As you read a play, you begin by trying to figure out the key ideas; what is the playwright saying? what are they exploring? what is their message? For example, a play might be about poverty and deal with ideas of economics, illness and injustice.

Criterion A of the production proposal assessment has two strands. One strand deals with ideas and the other deals with intentions.

The following activities are designed to help you identify and articulate the ideas and intentions in your chosen play text.

What is the play about?
Work with your chosen play text. There are two things to begin considering when you read a play text.

- ☑ The action—what happens in the play, the events or the storyline
- ☑ What the play is about—the themes of the play and what the playwright is trying to communicate

- Complete the prompts below using no more than 30 words for each.

What happens in the play is …

The play is about how …

Definition: Playwright
The playwright is the author of the play text. This might be one person, more than one person, or in some cases a theatre company.

Researching the background of the play

Research into a play text can be very useful after you have had an initial read and made up your own mind about the major themes. Research can give you information about when the play was written and about the playwright. This background can help you to think about the play in a new way.

Try to avoid researching previous productions of the play text as they might influence your ideas or restrict your vision.

Activity

Researching your play
- Carry out some research into the playwright and the background—when, how and why the play was written. Use the prompts below/opposite to help guide your research and use the spaces provided to capture your findings.

Capturing my research findings

What do you know about the playwright and their life? Did anything significant happen to the playwright that may have affected the subject or action of the play?

When was the play written? Did anything significant happen in the world at that time that may have influenced the subject or action of the play?

Where was the play written? Is there anything significant about the place
or its culture that may have affected the subject or action of the play?

Backstory and setting

Plays usually begin at a certain moment in time, so often the play will have some sort of
unseen "history"—events that happened before the play started and that influence the
action we see taking place in the play. We often find out about these events or action as
the play unfolds. We can call this the play's **backstory**.

The time and place in which the play takes place can also affect the action. This might
be because of social, political, or cultural events that have occurred in the world of the
play. We can call this the **setting**.

Exploring the past
- Using the space provided below, write a list of significant past events that
  have happened before the play begins.

This history of my chosen play	
Backstory	Setting

Definition: Climax of the play

This is the most decisive moment or turning point in the play text. This is usually the result of rising action in the play that leads to a heightened moment of tension or intense drama. It can often be the moment of most interest or engagement for the audience.

Top Tip

This type of chart can also be adapted to focus on an individual scene or can be used to show the journey of one specific character. It can become a useful tool for mapping specific moments of action prior to directing them.

Exploring structure

The structure of a play is how the playwright has ordered the action. It is the sequence of events or scenes as presented on stage to the audience. This structure gives the director a lot of information about how to pace the play—when to speed up, when to slow the action down—and when to fully capture the audience's attention.

The structure of a play, like a piece of music, provides a director with a shape to help them to think about how they are going to organize the audience's experience.

The following activity encourages you to identify the shape of the play you have chosen and to help you chart the moments of intensity for your audience.

Activity

The shape of the play

- Look through your play and choose the following.

  ☑ What you consider to be the moment of climax of the play
  ☑ Moments when there is a spike in the action
  ☑ Moments that are key to the subject/meaning/themes of the play

- Mark the moments with a dot (•) on the grid below. The high numbers are the point of most intensity.
- With a horizontal line (—) mark the action sections as follows.

  ☑ Where the action of the play slows down
  ☑ Where the action of the play speeds up
  ☑ Where nothing happens

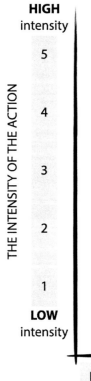

HIGH intensity

THE INTENSITY OF THE ACTION

5

4

3

2

1

LOW intensity

Beginning   Middle   End

TIMELINE OF THE PLAY

Opening and ending
The beginning/opening of a play is key because it introduces the audience to the world of the play and sets the mood.

The ending of the play is the final thing an audience experiences, so this is important. It can often communicate the final message of the play as well as leave the audience in a particular state of mind or with a specific feeling.

Comings and goings
- Look at the beginning/opening and the ending of your chosen play and consider the following questions.

  ☑ What sort of world is it at this particular moment?
  ☑ What is the mood at this particular moment?

- Use the space below to capture your thoughts and discoveries.

The world of my play

At the beginning/opening of the play

At the ending of the play

The key ideas

All the information you need regarding the key ideas of the play will be in the text; as mentioned earlier, you are looking for clues.

The ideas in a play text are usually communicated through the following features.

> Action: Events that take place and actions that the characters take
> Dialogue: What characters say or what is said about them
> Character: How characters behave
> Stage directions: Instructions regarding the setting or the action
> Situation: Circumstances people find themselves in
> Language: Words, images, descriptions, style, form (verse, prose, fragments) of writing used
> Setting: Geographical place(s), culture, period and specific locations where the action takes place

Top Tip

When you are writing your production proposal, you are encouraged to use quotes from the play to evidence your ideas, but be careful not to have big chunks of quotes as these take up valuable space and count towards the total number of words.

Activity

Clues in the text

- Read through your chosen play again and use the chart below to list all of the clues that you find in the text from each of the features described in the list above. These will help you to shape your understanding of the key ideas of the text.

Clue	Feature	Quote/explanation (include scene reference or page number)
	Action	
	Dialogue	
	Character	
	Stage directions	
	Situation	
	Language	
	Setting	

Activity

Targeting ideas
- Decide what you think might be the target idea(s) of the play. These are the ideas that you think lie at the heart of the play and the ones you will be making central to the production. You can think of this as the target for your production—these are the idea(s) you are aiming to communicate to the audience through your various artistic decisions.
- Using the diagram below, put the target ideas you think are central to the play in the centre. Put any other ideas that you think are key in the circle outside the centre.
- In the outermost circle you can put in ideas that only appear at certain moments in the play. These ideas aren't significant to the whole play.
- Use the evidence box to record how the ideas are presented in the play. This evidence might be from direct quotes, references or explanations from the play text to show how the ideas are being by the playwright.
- Feel free to create your own circles if you want to explore more ideas.

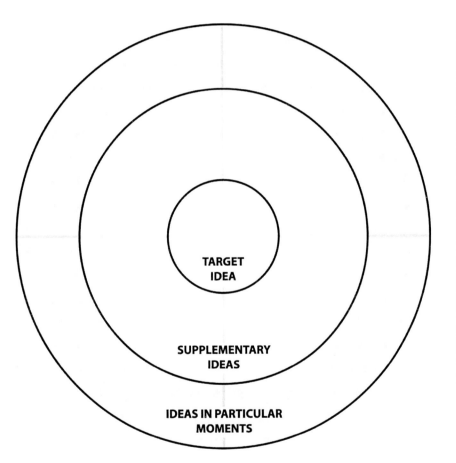

Evidence

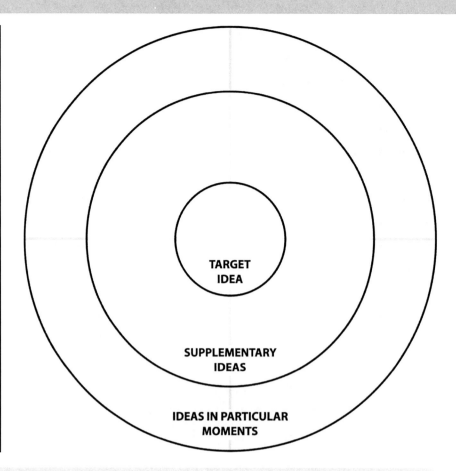

TARGET
IDEA

SUPPLEMENTARY
IDEAS

IDEAS IN PARTICULAR
MOMENTS

Activity

Explaining the ideas
- Explain the target idea(s) for the play. What do you think the playwright is saying? Explain how the playwright addresses these ideas using the list of clues you identified from the text earlier in this chapter.
- Think about how you would use this information when you stage the play.

Title of play text

Explanation of target idea(s)

How are the ideas addressed in the play text?

Top Tip
It is best to focus on fewer ideas and provide more detail. For example, if you think that a play is about power, you need to explain what power means, provide a detailed explanation of what the play is saying about power, and provide a detailed explanation of how the play is saying this about power.

3.4 Theatre-maker intentions

Your theatre-maker intentions are designed to provide you with a clear sense of how you imagine the play text will be presented to an audience, not as text, but as stage action. They also provide you with a clear idea of what you want the audience to experience and how you will create this experience using performance and production elements.

Beginning to visualize the play text in action
- As you begin to think about the play text, choose an image (drawn by you or sourced from elsewhere) to answer each of the questions below/overleaf. You can also add some additional notes to justify your choices.

Activity

Visualizing my play

If the play text was an object, which object would it be? Why?

If the play text was a piece of music, what sort of music would it be? Why?

If the play text was a piece of art in a gallery, what sort of piece would it be? Why?

Top Tip
Look back at the different types of theatre space in chapter 2 to see some examples of the more commonly used spaces.

The performance space

The performance space you choose to stage your play text in is very important. It can be any shape you choose it to be, and you can also choose to place the audience wherever you want.

Activity

Beginning to visualize the performance space
- Think of your chosen performance space as an empty box.
- Using the space provided opposite, draw the box to depict the outline of your chosen performance space. You will be using this drawing over the next few exercises to explore different ways of communicating your decisions about how the space will be used to stage your play and to communicate the ideas in the play text to an audience.

Top Tip
It is really important that you explicitly mention your choice of theatre space in your theatre-maker intentions as this is a requirement of the assessment task.

Settings

Depending on the play you have chosen, you will probably need your performance space to represent one or more of the following.

- One location
- Multiple locations
- An interior
- An exterior
- An existing place
- A fictional place

Thinking about which of these are relevant to your play will help you to decide the amount of space you need and how many different types of set you will need for each location. You also need to think about how and when any set pieces you use will be brought on and taken off. For example, does the scenery come in from the wings at the side of the stage? Is your set flown in from above? Does it stay in the performance space throughout the whole play? Does it come out of the floor? Is the space empty and different scenes are only depicted through the use of lights and special effects, such as projections?

My chosen performance space

Audience positioning and line of sight
The positioning of the audience is key to how the people watching your play will experience it.

As theatre-makers it is important to consider what the audience will see and from what direction. We call this the audience's **line of sight**. Here are some possibilities for positioning the stage action in relation to the audience's line of sight.

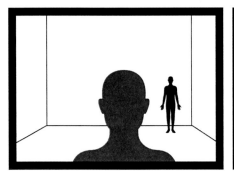

In the audience's direct eye line

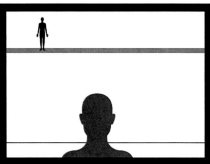

Above the audience

Below the audience

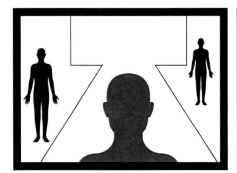

On either side of the audience

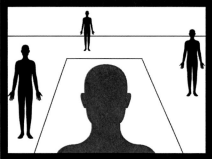

All around the audience

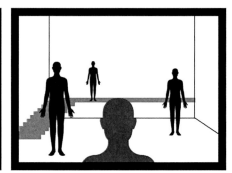

A combination of positions

Activity

Positioning your audience
- Decide on the positioning of your audience in relation to the performance space outline you completed in the previous activity. You can choose to position the audience wherever you want.
- Draw the audience in the box. You can use a series of symbols or markings to show the audience, such as those illustrated below.

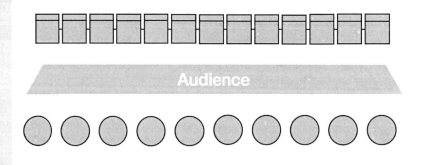

- In the space provided opposite, explain why you have chosen to position your audience in this way and how this affects their experience of the play.

Levels

In the staging of any play text, it is also important to consider levels. These sometimes help to avoid a play being one-dimensional. You can use pieces of staging to raise the action higher or set it lower and make the performance space more visually interesting or engaging. Below are some examples of how different levels are created on stage.

Techniques for creating levels on stage

	Stage blocks		Sunken pits
	Platforms on legs		Scaffold towers
	Staircases		High walkways
	Trapdoors in the stage floor		

Justification of my audience's position

Using levels on stage can often provide many possibilities for enhancing the on-stage action. They can be used to more clearly indicate different locations and can make the overall stage picture more dynamic and engaging.

Adding levels

- Add any levels you might want to use into your performance space box. These can be shown in different ways when you are developing your design ideas. For example, below is a set of stairs and a stage platform shown from above (plan view), from the side (section view) and as a 3D image. Choose whatever method of drawing works for you and your chosen approach.

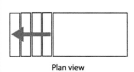

Plan view

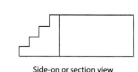

Side-on or section view

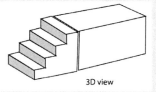

3D view

Performance styles

The performance style of a piece determines how the performers in a play will move, speak and act, as well as how they will be positioned. The style also often decides the design, style of the set and the production elements.

Many plays are written in a particular style or written to be performed in a particular style. As a director, however, you can choose to use a different style to bring the play to life, communicate its key ideas and give the audience an experience of the play that you think is most fitting. This is appropriate for this area of the syllabus, as long as you are clear why you have chosen this different style and can justify it. This task specifies that you must not change the text, but you are permitted to change features of the action. Sometimes the change to the performance style of the play might be because you have decided to change the setting or the period of the play. For example, you might decide to change the setting of a play from 18th century Spain to 20th century India or decide that a naturalistic play might be better presented as a piece of physical theatre.

Considering performance styles

Some of the most common theatrical performance styles are listed below.
- Carry out research into **four** different styles chosen from the following list.

  ☑ Naturalism   ☑ Physical theatre
  ☑ Epic theatre   ☑ Realism
  ☑ Expressionism   ☑ Symbolic
  ☑ Farce   ☑ Theatre of the absurd
  ☑ Grotesque   ☑ Theatre of cruelty
  ☑ Immersive

- Using the space provided, write a short definition of each of these four styles. An example has been completed for you.
- List how performers usually move, speak and are positioned in plays that are created in each chosen style.
- List how plays that are created in each chosen style usually make use of set, costume, lighting and sound.
- Describe the audience experience of plays that are created in each chosen style.
- Share your findings with others.

My research into theatrical performance styles	
Chosen style	➤ Realism
Definition	➤ Attempts to present the action of a play as if it is real and happening in front of you.
Use of performers	➤ Performers try to become the character—moving and speaking as if they are the character. Movements are based on the character's profile. ➤ Voice and speech patterns fit the character and are ones we can recognize—nothing artificial or exaggerated.
Use of set, costume, lighting and sound	➤ Costumes and setting are usually authentic to the period and place.
Audience experience	➤ The audience feels the action is really taking place and believes the actors.

Chosen style	
Definition	
Use of performers	
Use of set, costume, lighting and sound	
Audience experience	

Chosen style	
Definition	
Use of performers	
Use of set, costume, lighting and sound	
Audience experience	

Chosen style	
Definition	
Use of performers	
Use of set, costume, lighting and sound	
Audience experience	

Chosen style	
Definition	
Use of performers	
Use of set, costume, lighting and sound	
Audience experience	

Performance conventions

The choice of performance style can also determine the way a director decides how certain actions or directions in the play text will be consistently carried out on stage in the overall production. These are also called **performance conventions**, and these can be mentioned in your theatre-maker intentions as they affect the directing of the whole piece.

For example, a director might decide that the performers never leave the stage during the play, and that every time a character exits this is shown by the performer turning their back or that every time a particular character enters, the whole action freezes for two seconds.

Proxemics

The positioning of the performers in the space, in relation to objects in the space and in relation to each other, is also a useful tool for the director. This is known in theatre as proxemics. The spatial relationships of performers can communicate key ideas of the play as well as providing key information about character relationships, status and how characters relate to their environment.

How the performers relate to each other, to the space, to the objects in the space and to the audience is an interesting area to consider when directing a play text.

Reflection point
Proxemics is a huge area of study that considers how humans use space between themselves and others. Think about how you position yourself in the space around you when you are in the different environments you inhabit (school, home, bedroom, shop, public space). How do these environments affect how you use your body? Think about the different ways your body changes depending on where you are (e.g. basement), what is there (e.g. sealed boxes) and who you are with (someone you know well, a stranger, a close friend, a family member).

Experimenting with proxemics

Activity

- Carry out some improvisations using the list below as a prompt. Think about the effect each of these has on the audience and what ideas they may be communicating.

  - ☑ A character who always stands within easy reach of a particular chair
  - ☑ A character who never looks directly at any other character
  - ☑ A character who always stands in the centre of the space
  - ☑ A character who always keeps contact with the wall
  - ☑ A character who always turns their back when another character enters the space

Experimenting with performance styles

Activity

- With a partner choose **three** short excerpts (four or five lines) from different points in your chosen play. Using evidence in the text, define what you think might be the overall performance style of the play. Tell your partner what evidence there is to support why you think this is the case.
- Choose one of the excerpts and direct your partner using the performance style that you have selected. Consider how you would like your partner to use proxemics, their body and their voice in your chosen excerpt. For body and voice, be sure to consider each of the following.

Body
- ☑ Face
- ☑ Gesture
- ☑ Posture
- ☑ Body language
- ☑ Movement
- ☑ Manipulation of objects

Voice
- ☑ Volume
- ☑ Tone
- ☑ Emphasis
- ☑ Pace
- ☑ Pitch
- ☑ Pause
- ☑ Intonation
- ☑ Direction of voice
- ☑ Vocal characteristics (e.g. hesitation, lisp)

- Discuss with your partner how they used their body and voice to create a particular effect or communicate an idea or emotion.
- Using the same excerpt again, try directing it using a different performance style, which is appropriate to the play but contrasting to the chosen one.
- Choose a style that you think would be inappropriate for this particular text. Direct the same excerpt again but this time using this inappropriate performance style. What is the effect?
- Discuss with your partner how the choice of performance style changes each of the following.

  - ☑ The meaning of the piece
  - ☑ The experience of the audience
  - ☑ The organization of the space, positioning of the audience and production elements

Voicing your theatre-maker intentions
Using the activities above, record a short (two or three-minute) audio track of your theatre-maker intentions for the production of the play text. Imagine it's a pitch to a producer or funder, explaining your vision of the play and how you will bring it to life. Explain your ideas and your reasons for the artistic choices you are making.

3.5 Visual design ideas

Production elements are a key feature of staging a play as they are the scenic and technical elements used to transform a space into the world of the play. They create the look, feel and atmosphere of the realm that the performers are inhabiting.

This section of the production proposal task is about communicating your design ideas using visuals. Think of visuals as the language you are using to show what you have in your head when you think about staging the play. It gives the examiner an insight into your visual imagination.

For the next set of activities, we will now leave the play text you have been working on throughout this chapter and turn to a collection of excerpts that will give you the chance to experiment and think about different types of play texts.

Reflection and evaluation
The following script extracts present key moments from a variety of different plays.
- Read through each of the extracts and choose **two** that you would like to work on as a director/designer.

Script extract 1: Eurydice's women

In this epic play, commissioned for International Women's Day, an imprisoned prisoner of war, Eurydice, brings to life female characters from the classical Greek tragedies. The women each re-tell their experiences of war showing how their stories were distorted by the men who wrote the official histories of the conflict.

(A military camp in the heat. Dust. A piece of ragged silk is hoisted up as a shelter. Victors and victims.)

CASSANDRA:
You will die Agamemnon, you and your line will cease.

AGAMEMNON:
Take her away. Bind her mouth.

(Two soldiers enter. They tie CASSANDRA'S hands and bind her mouth. She cries as they take her away.)

Script extract 2: 18/11

In this expressionist drama following an explosion that killed her husband's family, the young woman who planned this murder finds herself alone with no memory of who she is or what has happened.

(Underground)

NESTRA:
I'm waiting. Waiting for him to arrive. Because I know he will. But I don't know who he is or why he's coming. I just know he's on his way. Then I see her. The little girl, the one who was sitting by the river. Over there. She's wearing a red dress with blue flowers and she's holding the old woman's hand. She's leading her through the corridors. What are they doing down here? Who are they?

(She calls.)

Hey. You.

Script extract 3: Excavations

The son and daughter of an archaeologist embark on a journey to discover their origins and the truth about the past. They encounter a series of grotesque characters who lead them to the difficult truths they will have to face.

(Lights on an elderly couple. They sit at a table preparing food—chopping, shredding, crushing.)

1: Before a birth, the food a mother eats must be made three days in advance.

2: And only by night.

1: An onion is chopped. The tears shed as each layer is peeled away are the liquid grief that the mother has suffered. The child will therefore be born happy.

2: Fresh almonds are crushed and mixed with a kilo of sugar. Spread under a pillow to release mother's dreams and the child will be freed from the prison of the womb.

Script extract 4: Arena

Commissioned for the opening of a new outdoor sculpture, this surreal play presents the complicated history of the site where the sculpture is located.

(A CLEANER is sweeping the space.)

WOMAN:
(Calling out) Arena! Arena!

(She notices the sweeper.)

WOMAN:
You busy?

CLEANER:
Sweep and brush. Nice and clean .

WOMAN:
It's so bright here.

CLEANER:
Flotsam, jetsam, sail and plank. Stuff they use to build the ships.

WOMAN
A spaceship. Yes.

CLEANER:
Time will tell.

WOMAN
Tick tock.

Script extract 5: Bloom

This immersive play was part of the London Cultural Olympiad. It deals with the story of a garden that a young woman has just inherited. The play is also a cultural history of gardening and our relationship to the landscape over time.

(We enter a composite garden. It is different periods of history simultaneously—1912, 1916, 1945, 1982 and 2012. GERTRUDE JEKYLL is painting the garden at an easel that is set up on a carpet of fake lawn. She is in her 70s and wears a long Edwardian dress finished off with solid gardening boots. Her face is half concealed by a battered and yellowed straw hat and two pairs of spectacles. In the centre of the lawn stands a tall sunflower and an old, antique-looking gnome. Objects left in the garden over time are also lying around. These include a china tea set, a peace pin and an old-fashioned pram. OS, with his back to us, is arranging a collection of gnomes. JAMES LANGLEY, in the uniform of a British First World War soldier, walks through the garden. Enter EMILY, the present-day owner of the garden.)

EMILY:
Can you all hear me at the back there? (She waits for a response.) Say if you can't. First of all thank you so much for coming here this evening, for volunteering your busy hands and precious time; without you, we just couldn't do it. Later tonight is the garden's grand opening and we want it to look tidy, yes tidy but also natural and a little bit outrageous. (She looks at the audience.) Now follow me, come this way.

(She leads the audience down a path. The sound of a chainsaw, trees and undergrowth being cleared drowns out her speech. High-pitched laughter of gnomes. She stops.)

Script extract 6: Body Talk

In this fast-paced comedy about gender, a group of friends try to figure out the identity of a mysterious body discovered in a lake.

TOM's VOICE:
I fell in love with them because they told stories. So maybe it wasn't really them I loved. They said the stories were real and we believed them—Ali, Emily, even Ryan. They were a good liar. We all were.

(TOM in a bridal gown. ALI is tacking it on.)

ALI:
Angel. That's what you are.

TOM:
So, how do I get to meet them? Tell me.

ALI:
Just go back.

TOM:
They won't be there. Pass the bottle.

ALI:
Don't spill any.

TOM:
What happens when brides spill their drink?

ALI:
Doesn't matter. They drink champagne.

TOM:
Doesn't champagne stain?

ALI:
Who cares? They keep the lights low.

TOM:
I could ask.

ALI:
Don't move. Asking won't help. Now stop wriggling or I'll end up sticking you full of pins.

Script extract 7: Faking it

In this tense thriller, a family receives news that their son has died in Arizona, USA. The young man's sister believes that he's still alive and travels to the US to find out the truth.

(The Arizona desert. Night. PRAN, a young man in his early twenties and ROBIN, slightly younger, are lying on the ground looking at the stars.)

PRAN:
I'm dead.

ROBIN:
How does it feel? To be dead.

PRAN:
It feels great. It feels brilliant.

ROBIN:
What time is it in Singapore?

PRAN:
About six. I don't want to think about Singapore.

ROBIN:
Do you want another drink? To celebrate.

PRAN:
No. Stay here.

ROBIN:
What?

PRAN:
You're always moving.

ROBIN:
I'll get my camera.

PRAN:
No. No camera. Look at the stars.

ROBIN:
They're amazing. Millions of them. They'd look great on film.

PRAN:
Do you know what they are, stars?

ROBIN:
Planets, aren't they?

PRAN:
Angels. Hovering above us, watching out for us. That's my one over there, blinking. They blink when they have messages.

ROBIN:
What's it saying?

Script extract 8: hIDe

A young vigilante group hunts for a young man with an assumed identity who has recently been released from prison. He committed a terrible crime when he was child that has affected them all.

BLAZE:
We was speeding along, 60, 70, hitting on 80
Me, Speed and The Hoax
The windows open and - feel the wind
Roar
I think, we're gonna crash and I'm gonna die
And then I think, so what?
Who cares?
I'm gonna die and I love this.
This is free
Like you've never been before

SPEED:
And then we see it
The blue
On–off light
Cops
Neon and sirens screaming
Just like in the films

BLAZE:
"Foot down, Speed"
I says
"Foot down, let's beat them"

SPEED:
Cops getting closer and then …

BLAZE:
Quick
Turn left
No
Right
Go

SPEED:
Riding over the pavement
People running

BLAZE:
Go Speed
Go

SPEED:
Blaze here screaming

BLAZE:
Faster Speed
Go, faster
Me
No breath in me lungs

SPEED:
Car stops
Jump out

BLAZE:
Run, run

SPEED:
Blaze running
Hear the cops behind us
Big boots like an army

BLAZE:
Running
Lights
Turn down
Alley bins go flying
Turn again
Hoax
Where are you?

SPEED:
Keep running
Shops whiz
Wind rush

BLAZE:
Cops on the tail
Turn

Turn again
Alley
Road
Hide behind someone's wall

SPEED:
Made it

BABY BLUE:
Sure no one followed?

BLAZE:
We've lost Hoax

Script extract 9: Leaves on a line

A comedy drama in two parts that takes place at a train station. One part tells the story of a young child (FEN) abandoned on the line and the woman (LENA) who found and adopted him. The other part tells the story of the birth mother (LI) who left him there.

(A large screen resembling a departure and arrivals board. There is a raised area downstage made of three blocks on which FEN is about to build a miniature railway. FEN controls a video camera that projects live images onto the screen. There are also two microphones on stands that the characters use for narration. Lights up on LENA with a suitcase. She opens it. The suitcase releases its memory, lighting up her face with a white November light, the sound of a station, steam. As she speaks, a miniature figure of a girl such as you would find on a miniature railway appears on the screen.)

LENA:

It's 1963. I'm four. Father's taking me on a steam train for its final journey. It's November. The train's crowded and, as we get off, I'm separated from my father, swept along with the crowd onto the platform. (The sound of seagulls.) I can't see him anywhere. Strangers mourning the train's last journey tower above me. I'm miniature, tiny, afraid, gulls circle and cry. When eventually he finds me, he lifts me up onto his shoulders and the world stretches out below me. I hold on but nothing makes it better. And it's been like that ever since. Fear on my shoulder, like, like some huge bird—screeching, into my ear, reminding me that everything, everything can be lost in a single moment.

(While LENA speaks LI enters and begins drawing a line across the space from left to right.)

LI:

A line begins at X and moves continuously towards Y. Lines have no depth or breadth, no fear or hesitation; they are simply movements that take you away from one thing and towards another. The skill of drawing a straight line lies in your ability to always look ahead, fixed on your destination, ignoring the point of departure.

Script extract 10: Raving

A highly physical, contemporary rewrite of The Bacchae *by Euripides set in the contemporary clubbing scene, exploring political oppression and the desire to escape a world where you do not fit in.*

(A place that is both nightclub and classical underworld, interior and exterior, where time does not exist, an everlasting present)

DIO:
What do you with a bad kid? The type of kid your mamma warned you about.

You dance with them, that's what, keeping your eyes fixed on their eyes, keeping track of their heartbeat until their heartbeat becomes a track you're dancing to. Watch them until they begin to blur, out of focus with no hard edges to trip over or fall off. All blur. And you fall towards them and somehow, they catch you and you find yourself in a place where everything is clear, and nothing is obvious.

You've become a shadow.

That's what love does. It turns you into a shadow.

CHORUS:
Darkness and shadow
Catching and falling
Edges and borders

Slipping through them all

Not hidden in containers or lorries

Dio is a god who walks past guards and officials
Without the need of passports or papers

Bullets fly past and bombs don't fall near

Dio dances to the whiz of the aircraft
Skips over landmines
Dio
A sixteen-year-old god
Child of fire
Born out of a lightning bolt

Articulating a vision for staging

Think about how you would stage the two excerpts you have chosen in two contrasting performance spaces with two different audience positions.

- Using the spaces provided overleaf, draw the shape of the space and position your audience in it. Mark the audience's line of sight.
- Draw in any levels you might want to use.
- Add other lines and shapes to indicate any items of set that you would like to use. Provide a note of what each line/shape represents and its approximate dimensions.
- Indicate where any performers are positioned at the start of the section you have chosen, using an X to represent them.
- Provide any other information you think is relevant.
- Share your designs with a partner and justify the choices you have made, referring to the target ideas for the sections of play text you have chosen.

Reflection point

Think about how different plays suggest a different:
- type of audience experience
- type of space
- audience positioning
- use of production and performance elements.

Performance space for chosen excerpt 1

Script extract No: Title:

Performance space for chosen excerpt 2

Script extract No: Title:

Activity

Staging in action
- Now choose just **one** of the two excerpts you worked with in the previous exercise.
- Mark out the rough area of the performance space in your classroom workspace. You can use tape or chairs to mark the shape of the space and where the audience sits. Use chairs, pieces of furniture or staging (if you have any available) to create any levels you are using.
- Working with others in your class, stage the excerpt you have chosen.
- After experimenting with practically staging the excerpt, write down responses to the following questions in the reflection space provided below.

  ☑ How does the space and audience position affect the movement and speech of the performers in this piece?
  ☑ What effect might the space and audience position have on the audience's experience of this piece?
  ☑ How you think the target idea of the piece is being communicated?

- Repeat the above exercise but move the performance space to a different room or space. Set up the position of the audience in a completely different way.
- After experimenting with practically staging the excerpt in the new space, use the boxes provided below/opposite to write a short reflection on how you think the choice of performance space and audience positioning affects or alters:

  ☑ the audience's experience of this piece
  ☑ the way the performers move and speak in this piece
  ☑ the meaning of the play.

- Discuss your findings with a partner.

Reflections on the use of performance space 1

Reflections on the use of performance space 2

Production elements and the visual production design ideas

When working on your production proposal, it is important that the production elements you choose to employ in your staging are the best ones for meeting your theatre-maker intentions and that the examiner is clear why you have made your choices.

This section will help you explore production elements in more depth and consider some of the different ways of communicating their use to the examiner through visuals.

Different production elements can be combined to create the world of the play for an audience. These elements include the following.

- Organization of space
- Set
- Props
- Costume
- Sound
- Lighting
- Special effects

Your production proposal must include visual production ideas that show your vision for the overall play, and not just for individual moments. These visuals must be created with care and must clearly communicate your ideas. These visuals can include any of the following.

 Diagrams

 Photographs

Drawings

 Plans

 Collages

 Mood boards

Paintings

 Photographs of a 3D model box you have created

 Sourced images from the internet/books/magazines (be sure to keep a record of the sources as these are required)

Bringing the Arizona desert to life in a production proposal

Let us consider how a specific location might be presented visually in a production proposal. For the purposes of this exercise, the chosen location is the Arizona desert in the USA.

This location could be presented through a variety of visuals. Below are some examples.

A photograph

Credit: Andrew Ruiz (2022) on Unsplash.com

An aerial plan

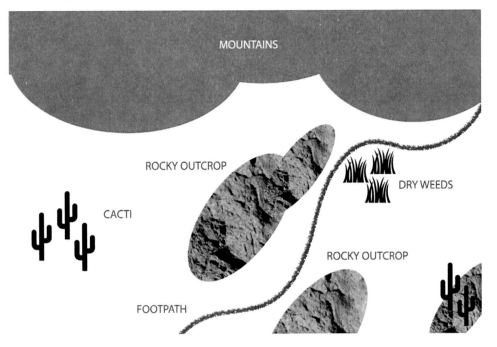

MOUNTAINS

ROCKY OUTCROP

DRY WEEDS

CACTI

ROCKY OUTCROP

FOOTPATH

> **Top tip**
> These example production ideas have all been created digitally. The production proposal task, however, can be successfully completed using only hand-drawn images or a combination of digital and analogue techniques. It is your production proposal, so make the most of whichever approach works best for you.

A 3D drawing

White backdrop

Cut-out flats of mountains

Cut-out flats of cacti

Raised platforms

Cut-outs of dry grass

A detail of a set piece (e.g. a flat)

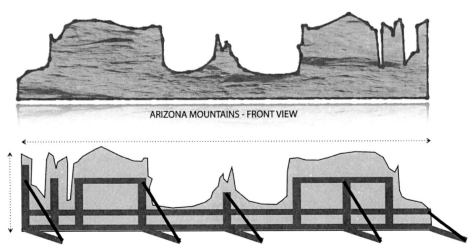

ARIZONA MOUNTAINS - FRONT VIEW

ARIZONA MOUNTAINS - REAR VIEW

A lighting diagram

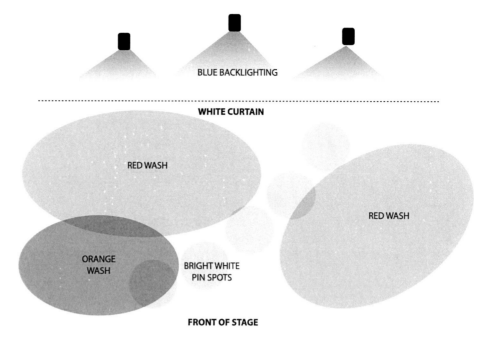

The following exercises encourage you to start experimenting with ways of visually communicating your own production ideas on paper.

Communicating production ideas visually
Below/opposite is a smaller selection of the script extracts you explored earlier, with only the stage directions presented. Each script has also been provided with a clearly defined theatre-maker intention.

- Read through the stage directions and theatre-maker intentions at the start of each extract.
- Choose two of the extracts that have contrasting settings and theatre-maker intentions that appeal to you.
- Using the space provided overleaf, experiment with creating different types of visuals to show your design ideas for each extract. These should include:

  - ☑ the overall set
  - ☑ the lighting
  - ☑ a costume
  - ☑ a key prop/piece of scenery.

- Share your ideas with a partner.
- Based on what you had to describe and explain to your partner, add a caption to each of your drawings to provide any detail that was not clear from looking at the visual alone. If you used found images, make sure that you have attributed the sources below the images.
- Add text in the boxes provided to explain your production ideas and how they are used to meet the stated intentions for each piece.

Eurydice's women

A military camp in the heat. Dust. A piece of ragged silk is hoisted up as a shelter. Victors and victims.

Intentions	(Staged in the round. A feeling of threat, stories are subversive, audience are co-conspirators, a world both modern and ancient, idea of war and conflict being a never-ending cycle of violence. Performance style uses elements of classical Greek tragedy as well as a more expressionist style.

Raving

A place that is both nightclub and classical underworld, interior and exterior, where time does not exist, an everlasting present.

Intentions	Staged in a warehouse. A feeling of being in another world, of being transported out of your surroundings; this play is about subcultures. This is a piece about young people and their lives and the way they are controlled by a political system run by adults. Clubbing is a space of freedom and power. The audience needs to feel transported from one world to another through the club world. Performance style is highly physical with moments of physical theatre and dance combined.

Leaves on a line

A large screen resembling a departure and arrivals board. There is a raised area downstage made of three blocks on which FEN is about to build a miniature railway. FEN controls a video camera that projects live images onto the screen. There are also two microphones on stands that the characters use for narration. Lights up on LENA with a suitcase. She opens it. The suitcase releases its memory, lighting up her face with a white November light, the sound of a station, steam. As she speaks, a miniature figure of a girl such as you would find on a miniature railway appears on the screen.

Intentions	Thrust stage. A memory play about how the past always finds a way of surfacing in the present. A nostalgic atmosphere and the sense of how we go on journeys that take us to the past and how the past can carry us into the future. Using different storytelling techniques and bringing together theatre, film, visual art and music. Performance style is varied, borrowing from different art forms and from storytelling techniques from different cultures.

Faking it

The Arizona desert. Night. PRAN, a young man in his early twenties and ROBIN, slightly younger, are lying on the ground looking at the stars.

Intentions	Proscenium stage. A play about the complex nature of families and the need sometimes to escape to find freedom. A melancholic piece that moves between two continents and two different worlds. Audience feels sympathetic towards each of the characters. This piece is naturalistic in performance style.

Bloom

We enter a composite garden. It is different periods of history. simultaneously—1912, 1916, 1945, 1982 and 2012. GERTRUDE JEKYLL is painting the garden at an easel which is set up on a carpet of fake lawn. She is in her 70s and wears a long Edwardian dress finished off with solid gardening boots. Her face is half concealed by a battered and yellowed straw hat and two pairs of spectacles. In the centre of the lawn stands a tall sunflower and an old, antique-looking gnome. Objects left in the garden over time are also lying around. These include a china tea set, a peace pin and an old-fashioned pram. OS, with his back to us, is arranging a collection of gnomes. JAMES LANGLEY, in the uniform of a British First World War soldier, walks through the garden. Enter EMILY, the present-day owner of the garden.

Intentions	Promenade. A mixture of interior of a house and exterior garden and grounds. An immersive piece where the audience is in the heart of the garden. A piece about how the landscape changes around us, how we try to control it and how nature has a way of fighting back. Also, a celebration of gardens and our connection to nature. The performance style is a mixture of realistic and exaggerated, and symbolism is used extensively.

Visual design ideas for extract 1

Title:

Caption

Visual design ideas for extract 2

Title:

Caption

Explaining my production ideas (extract 1)

Explaining my production ideas (extract 2)

3.6 Staging moments of tension, emotion, atmosphere and/or meaning

We can think of a play text as being made up of a series of moments of tension, emotion, atmosphere and/or meaning ("TEAM"). All of these moments together create the full text and make up the audience experience.

The first thing to do is to identify moments of "TEAM" in the play and then choose **one** of them to work with. This section of the production proposal is about focusing on a specific moment and showing how you would direct this moment using performance and production elements. This section needs to be incredibly detailed. Whereas the section on visual design is about the **overall** production, this is about a **particular** instance in the play.

You are now going to work with the excerpts you chose earlier from a full script and explored. Consider each of your selected excerpts as a moment of "TEAM". Selecting the moment of "TEAM" from the play is a key part of this exercise.

Choosing a moment of "TEAM"
With a partner, read through each of the full script excerpts you explored earlier in this chapter.
- Identify whether each excerpt is a moment of "TEAM". Even though a moment might include more than **one** aspect of "TEAM", you need to decide on only one that you think is the main feature of the moment.
- Discuss what you think makes it a moment of "TEAM" as you read through the excerpts.
- Choose one moment to work on. Write a list of the ingredients in the text that has made you decide this moment conveys tension, emotion, atmosphere or meaning. You can write this directly onto the script itself.
- Imagine what happened just before this moment and just after this moment.
- Discuss how the 'before' and the 'after' affects the moment.

Performance elements
The production proposal assessment criteria require you to think about creating "TEAM" in a chosen moment through the use of performance elements.

The next activity extends the work on a selected moment from the activity above.

Using performance elements to communicate "TEAM"
- Whichever one of the four aspects of "TEAM" you chose to explore in the chosen script extract in the previous activity, create a photo/video catalogue of performance elements of:

  ☑ gestures that create this aspect (e.g. if it is a moment of tension, you will catalogue gestures of tension)
  ☑ body shapes that create this aspect
  ☑ movements that create this aspect
  ☑ positioning(s) in relationship to another person that create this aspect
  ☑ positioning(s) in relationship to a prop or set that create this aspect..

- With a partner or in a small group, photograph yourselves in position for three parts of the moment—the beginning, the middle and the end. Think about the performance elements you catalogued above. Can you use any of these? You might also want to think about what happens just before and just after the moment.

- Using the spaces provide below/overleaf, turn these photographs into three sketches/drawings with explanations.
- Find someone who did not work with you on this or who is not in your class.
- Using the three sketches explain how performance elements create your chosen aspect of "TEAM" in this moment. Keep a note of anything that was not clear in your explanation. This will help you to think about what further information you might need to include in your actual production proposal to make your ideas clear to an examiner.

Sketch 1: The beginning

Sketch 2: The middle

Sketch 3: The end

Production elements

The arrangement and use of the performance space along with production elements (as well as the performance elements) also play a key role in creating "TEAM". In this section of your production proposal, you can explain the way that performance and production elements work **together** to create the moment.

Using production elements to communicate "TEAM"
- Building on the work you did in the previous activity, decide what music or sound effects you would like to use in your moment to create the desired effect and at which point in the text sound will be used.
- Make a recording of you reading the text whilst playing the sound(s) in the background.
- Think about other production elements and how you could use them to create the desired effect.
- Play the recording a few times; each time you listen to it draw a quick sketch of the following, in this order, on a large piece of paper.

  ☑ The shape of the performance space and audience positioning
  ☑ Any set—set pieces, staging, levels, furniture/objects, floor cloth
  ☑ The lights, their position, colour, intensity and range

- Take the sketches of figures from the previous exercise and draw costume ideas over these using colour, items of clothing, accessories, texture.
- Put your drawings of production elements alongside the performance sketches and take note of how the performance and production elements work together to create the moment of "TEAM".
- Video yourself making a presentation explaining how you will direct/design this moment using performance and production elements to create "TEAM".

3.7 Preparing for assessment: Structuring your production proposal

When it comes to completing your production proposal, the examiner wants to see a variety of skills and understandings related to transforming a play text into live action.

You need to structure your production proposal carefully to ensure you give consideration to the criteria weighting for each area. Your completed production proposal should adhere to the following structure.

1. **Ideas and intentions** (8 marks)
   a. Each student explains the key ideas presented in the entire play text. With close reference to the play text, using specific examples from the text to support their explanations.

   Recommended maximum length: 2 pages

   b. Each student uses their interpretation of the play text to develop and explain their theatre-maker intentions for the staging of the entire play.

   Recommended maximum length: 2 pages

2. **The proposed design** (4 marks)
   The student presents their production designs visually with an explanation and justification of the performance space and how they would employ production elements to meet their stated theatre-maker intentions. These are overarching

design proposals for the look and feel of the production as a whole rather than a detailed analysis of any specific moments in the play.

Recommended maximum length: 4 pages

3. **The proposed staging of one moment of the play** (8 marks)
Each student envisions how they would stage one specific moment in the play, explaining how they would use both performance and production elements in this moment of the play to effectively create tension, emotion, atmosphere, and/or meaning (or "TEAM"). These are detailed proposals for staging one specific moment in fulfilment of the theatre-maker intentions. As students are expected to discuss both performance and production elements in this section they must be sure to fully justify the exclusion of either one if they choose to eliminate them from their vision for the staging of the specific moment (for example, the removal of performers from the space entirely, or the staging of a moment without the use of any set or lighting).

Recommended maximum length: 4 pages

Assessment criteria
The assessment criteria for the production proposal are as follow.

Production proposal assessment criteria
Criterion A: Ideas and intentions
Evidence: production proposal

   i.   To what extent does the student explain the ideas addressed by the chosen play text, with reference to the play text?
   ii.   To what extent does the student explain their intentions of the staging of the entire play?

What the examiner wants to see
Criterion A(i)
- Your understanding of the play and of the ideas it deals with
- That you are able to provide a detailed explanation of each of the key ideas and how the playwright is dealing with these ideas
- That you are able to offer a justification and evidence from the play to prove this

Criterion A(ii)
- **Your interpretation of the key ideas of the play**
 This is what you think is the heart of the play. Here you need to explain the idea in the play (e.g. "One of the key ideas the play deals with is the damage war does to community and how …"), then explain your interpretation of this idea (e.g. "For me, the play is about how in times of war everyone becomes so concerned with themselves that community breaks down, so I want to focus on the individual stories of each character and bring those to life.").

- **Your decisions on how you will stage your interpretation and the effect you want this to have on your audience**

  The effect you want the play to have on the audience is going to be key to all your decisions. The audience effect will be based on what you want the audience to feel, as well as how you want them to think about the play. You need to provide a lot of detail as to how you want the audience to experience the play, why you think this is appropriate for the play and how you plan to create this effect. It is worth thinking about this section as also being about what you want the audience to leave with at the end of the performance. You might also want to think about the senses and how these might contribute to the experience—for example, what would it mean to have the audience sitting on uncomfortable seats or in a space that is overheated?

- **Your chosen performance space**

  Your choice of performance space and positioning of the audience needs to be explained in reference to the audience experience. Where the audience is positioned and the performer and audience relationship, effected by the space, is key to both the experience of the audience and the performance style. Explaining the nature of the space is key here—dimensions, sense of space (for example, intimate, spacious, cavernous), shape of the space, positioning of performance area, the colour scheme of the space. You might want to choose an already existing space, but still be sure to explain what it is like and why you have chosen it.

- **Your chosen performance style**

  This is about explaining the overall performance style of the play and why you have chosen this as the main style. Connect it to the audience experience and also to the ideas of the play. Sometimes you might choose a performance style that is different to the style the play is written in. Make sure you explain what this style is as well as why you have chosen it. Even if you stick with the style of the play, make sure you explain what the style is, why you have decided to keep it and how this will contribute to the audience experience.

- **Your decisions about how you will use performance and production elements to stage your interpretation**

  This is about how you will use performance and production elements to
     a.   communicate what you think are the key ideas of play (your interpretation)
     b.   create the experience you want the audience to have.
  This section is about showing how performance and production elements are used for both of these purposes.

Production proposal assessment criteria
Criterion B: The proposed design
Evidence: production proposal

   i.   To what extent does the student present their visual production design ideas with an explanation of how these will be used to achieve their intentions in the staging of the entire play?

What the examiner wants to see
Criterion B(i)

- That you refer closely to your theatre-maker intentions as explained in criterion A.
- Your explanation of how production elements will be used to meet your stated theatre-maker intentions.
- Your explanation of how you will use production elements to turn your intentions into action
- Your production design ideas presented through visuals that are clear, neat and have been carefully put together.

Production proposal assessment criteria
Criterion C: The proposed staging of one moment of the play
Evidence: production proposal

i. To what extent does the student explain how they would use **performance** elements to effectively create tension, emotion, atmosphere and/or meaning ("TEAM") in one specific moment they have chosen to stage?

ii. To what extent does the student explain how they would use **production** elements to effectively create tension, emotion, atmosphere and/or meaning ("TEAM") in one specific moment they have chosen to stage

What the examiner wants to see
Criterion C(i) and C(ii)

- That you provide explanation of why the particular moment you have selected is a moment of "TEAM"—it is best to choose a moment that is no more than one or two aspects of "TEAM", at most, otherwise you might not be providing enough detail
- That you can focus on the moment—although you might also refer to what happens just before and what happens just after, as this might also influence the audience's experience
- That you provide an explanation of your theatre-maker intentions for this particular moment. These might be different to your overall intentions for the whole play (for example, in a play about war, this moment might be a moment of peace and you may want to create this as a contrast to the overall feel of the play)
- That you offer an explanation of how you will use performance elements to turn the moment of "TEAM" in the text into an experience and how this affects the audience (an effect of tension/emotion/atmosphere and/or meaning) when it is staged
- That you offer an explanation of how you will use production elements to turn the moment of "TEAM" in the text into an experience and how this affects the audience (an effect of tension/emotion/atmosphere and/or meaning) when it is staged. You might also want to use visuals if these will help your explanations.

Chapter 3: Recap

In this chapter we have explored the topic of staging play texts and the production proposal, focusing on:

- choosing a play text that ignites the imagination and offers a wealth of theatrical potential for staging

- identifying and exploring the ideas presented by a playwright in a play text

- formulating precise theatre-maker intentions that include consideration of the performance space and the performance style

- communicating visual design ideas on the page through a variety of different approaches

- identifying moments of "TEAM" and approaches to staging these through both performance and production elements

- structuring the production proposal for assessment.

4. Exploring world theatre traditions and the research presentation

You can either work individually, in pairs or in small groups for all of the activities in this chapter.

Introduction

This chapter addresses the following areas of exploring world theatre traditions.

4.1   Academic integrity and presentations
4.2   Researching world theatre traditions
4.3   Researching a performance convention
4.4   The practical exploration of a performance convention
4.5   Experimenting with traditional performance material
4.6   Reflecting on learning
4.7   Preparing for assessment: Structuring and recording your presentation

The exploring world theatre traditions syllabus area characterizes the international nature of theatre as a DP subject within the IB. It encourages you to go beyond your familiar theatrical knowledge and to be open to encountering and learning something outside your comfort zone. In a lot of ways, the less you know about a tradition, the more likely you are to find the experience authentically eye-opening and interesting. The experience of learning about theatre traditions from around the world also gives you the opportunity to learn about different cultures, their attitudes to theatre and the role performance plays in their communities. The cultural context of the theatre traditions you explore is key to your understanding of theatre from around the world and to the development of your perspectives as an internationally minded theatre-maker.

> **Definition: Theatre tradition**
> A theatre tradition is defined as a theatre practice that has a fixed set of specific performance conventions that have not changed significantly over time.

In this respect, you will be exploring something from around the world that has remained largely unchanged. These traditions are forms of performance that have been experienced by different audiences and that have survived the test of time and the challenges of globalization. Many have been passed down through generations—orally, through written materials, through training programmes, through apprenticeships and through observation.

It is these **traditional performance conventions**, these particular and fixed ways of performing through the body and voice, that allow you to encounter not only something from a tradition that has remained constant over time but also the skill set of performers in other parts of the world. Using both academic research and your own physical explorations, you will come to understand how these skills are used in traditional performances as well as how you can use them to develop your own skills.

> **Definition: Performance convention**
> A performance convention is a significant and identifiable element of performance (body and/or voice) that is usually culturally recognized, accepted and identified as a key feature of the theatre tradition.

Reflection point

Carry out some research into somatic learning and consider how you might develop your capacity to learn through the body in theatre. In what areas, other than theatre, might this be an effective form of learning? How might you learn from other physically based areas of knowledge?

Developing as a performer is a key part of this task, so you will be approaching this from the perspective of the performer. Thinking about this syllabus area as a form of performance training that will also help you with contemporary performance means that you can think of exploring theatre traditions from around the world as a relevant and useful resource rather than the study of something foreign or "other".

Learning in this task is through the body—known as somatic learning. The idea behind this is that understanding and knowledge in theatre often resides within the body. Exploration and experimentation through the body and/or voice is regarded as a powerful and important way of developing understanding. Research in theatre, therefore, is very often physical. It is still important to conduct academic research, but in theatre research it is often the application of academic research to practical work that produces the most significant discoveries. The research presentation task encourages this—inviting you to explore, experiment and reflect on your learning through your body and voice as performers, and as students of theatre.

Overall, exploring world theatre traditions is an area of the syllabus that is designed to expand your perspectives, broaden your theatrical experience, and develop you as a performer and as an internationally minded learner. It requires you to be an inquisitive explorer, embarking on a journey of exploration through the body into the unfamiliar. As a significant encounter with the unfamiliar, there will be challenges and rewards that will shape the outcomes of this learning experience. Think of this task as a carefully considered and respectful "opening-the-door" experience in search of cultural insight and creative inspiration, appreciating that to master the skills of the world theatre traditions prescribed in this task would take many years and, in many cases, require total immersion in the culture from which the tradition arises.

What the guide says

For the research presentation assessment task each student is required to submit the following.
- A video recording of the student's research presentation (15 minutes maximum).
- A list of all sources cited and any additional resources used by the student during the presentation.

This task requires you to video record a presentation of your processes and discoveries whilst undertaking the following.

- Select and carry out research into an unfamiliar theatre tradition, which must be selected from the list of prescribed traditions in the Theatre guide.
- Identify one performance convention from the theatre tradition that you wish to explore in more depth.
- Research the performance convention you have selected.
- Identify the performance aspect(s) (face, voice, gesture, posture movement and/or manipulation of objects) you wish to employ to guide your practical exploration of the chosen convention.
- Undertake a process of practical exploration in order to develop an understanding of the performance convention through the body and/or voice.
- Identify how the performance convention is used in traditional performance material from the tradition.
- Choose performance material from the tradition where the convention features.
- Use the performance material to experiment with the convention.
- Reflect on the processes you have undertaken and your discoveries.

- Reflect on how the practical exploration of the performance convention has contributed to your development as a performer.
- Consider how your inquiry into the chosen theatre tradition has further developed your understanding of theatre in the world.
- Put together your list of sources and any other resources you have used.

Assessment criteria
The research presentation is assessed using the following criteria.

	Research presentation	Marks	Total
A	The unfamiliar theatre tradition	8	
B	Practical exploration of the performance convention	8	24
C	Reflection on learning	8	

The activities outlined in this chapter have been designed to fully prepare you for success in each of these areas.

4.1 Academic integrity and presentations

The name of the assessment task for this syllabus area—the research presentation—highlights the significance that research plays in this task. As mentioned above, there are two forms of research that this syllabus area deals with: academic research and research through practice.

Academic research is most commonly conducted through the following.

- Consulting sources
- Observation
- Collecting and analysing data

Research through practice may be conducted through your own body or by observing other bodies in action. It is research that is most commonly conducted through the following.

- Physical activities and exercises
- Practical exploration
- Physical experimentation

It is important that you keep track of whatever sources you use for your inquiries. You should also keep a record of whatever method(s) you choose to follow in order to arrive at your conclusions. These will be required to show that you have conducted research with academic integrity.

In an oral presentation, attributing sources, providing evidence and sharing the basis of new-found understandings is more challenging than in a traditional written essay. This is a challenge that you will have to overcome for this assessment task, so you will need to think about and develop the skills of attributing sources in an oral presentation.

Activity

Academic integrity

- Read the section below from the *Theatre guide* and using the space provided, identify the key features of academic integrity for this task.

Key features of academic integrity

Academic integrity

Students must ensure their assessment work adheres to the IB's academic integrity policy and that all sources are appropriately referenced. When orally presenting in this assessment task, students must clearly distinguish between their words and those of others by either verbally stating a citation or through the use of a visual cue, such as a reference on a keynote slide. This must occur at the point of use in the presentation to ensure there is no doubt when work is attributed to another person. A student's failure to appropriately acknowledge a source will be investigated by the IB as a potential breach of regulations that may result in a penalty imposed by the IB Final Award Committee. See the "Academic integrity" section of this guide for full details.

Definition: Citation

A citation is a reference to a source that you have used for your research. This can include a quotation from, or reference to, a book, interview, author or academic paper, for example. A citation enables your readers to locate the sources you consulted and is a way of supporting and verifying your research as accurate.

Activity

Attributing sources in an oral presentation

- Different types of research source require different approaches to citation. Find out what the chosen referencing style of your school is (for example, Harvard) and carry out research into how to orally cite different research sources when presenting.
- In the space provided below/opposite, write up a list of best practice guidelines to help with attributing sources in an oral presentation, along with suggestions of the various ways you might do it.
- Consider the types of sources presented in the table opposite and write ideas for how you might orally cite them in an oral presentation. Also, consider different ways of introducing your research—for example, using phrases such as "According to …" or "In their interview with…".

Best practice for attributing sources in an oral presentation

Type of research sources	How to orally cite this source
Books	
Journals	
Documents (archive)	
Newspapers/magazines	
Websites	
Filmed/audio interviews or accounts	
Diaries	
Videos	
Podcasts	
Face-to-face interviews (in person or online)	

This chapter includes research into Kathakali dance theatre that was written by Fenella Kelly, an expert and performer of this theatre tradition. Her work has been informed by the following sources, which are presented in APA format.

Kathakali dance theatre: List of sources
Appukuttan, N., & Panikar, K. A. (1993). *Kathakali: The art of the non-worldly*. Marg Publications. Balkrishnan, S. (2004). *Kathakali*. Wisdom Tree. Gopalakrishnan, K. K. (2016). *Kathakali dance-theatre*. Niyogi Books. Namboodiripad, N. C. (2012). *Revealing the art of natyasastra*. Munshiram Manoharlal Publishers Ltd. Pandeya, A. C. (1999). *The art of kathakali*. Munshiram Manoharlal Publishers Ltd. Rangacharya, A. (2005). *Introduction to Bharata's natyasastra*. Munshiram Manoharlal Publishers Ltd. Sucheendran, V. S. (2022). *Personal interview*. Kerala Kathakali Centre manager, Fort Cochin, India. Venu, G. (2000). *The language of kathakali*. Natana Kairali.

4.2 Researching world theatre traditions

The *Theatre guide* provides a prescribed list of theatre traditions for you to choose from for the research presentation assessment task. The tradition you choose for your final assessment must not be one that you have previously studied in depth, but it is important to carry out some background research into each of the prescribed traditions to identify one that interests you.

World theatre traditions prescribed by the *Theatre guide*

Rating	World theatre tradition	Geographical location
	17th century French farce	France
	Barong (or Rangda) dance	Indonesia
	British pantomime	United Kingdom
	Cantonese, Yueju, or Peking opera (Jingju)	China
	Commedia dell'arte	Italy
	Elizabethan theatre	England
	Hun lakhon lek puppetry	Thailand
	Jatra	Bangladesh
	Kabuki	Japan
	Karagoz shadow puppetry	Turkey
	Kathakali	India

	Kecak	Indonesia
	Khon dance drama	Thailand
	Kyogen farce	Japan
	Nautanki	India
	Noh theatre	Japan
	Pastorela	Mexico
	Punch and Judy puppets	United Kingdom
	Rakugo "sit down" theatre	Japan
	Talchum mask dance	Korea
	Topeng dance	Bali
	Victorian melodrama	England
	Wayang golek puppetry	Indonesia, Malaysia
	Wayang kulit shadow puppetry	Indonesia, Malaysia

Familiarity test and "what appeals?"

- Look through the list of prescribed theatre traditions provided above and allocate a number rating for each tradition (in the column provided) to indicate your level of familiarity. Use the rating system as follows.

  1. I am completely unfamiliar with the tradition
  2. I have some basic knowledge of the tradition
  3. I am broadly familiar with the tradition
  4. I am very familiar with the tradition

- Looking back through your ratings, identify three traditions that you have marked between 1 and 3 that you think would be interesting to research further.
- Carry out research into each of the chosen theatre traditions and the cultural context of each, to get a general idea of the tradition and its associated practices. Record this in the table overleaf. What does this theatre tradition look and sound like in performance? What is a performer required to do in this theatre tradition?
- Make sure you record all of the sources you consult while carrying out this research.
- For each of the researched traditions, write a brief explanation of what does and does not appeal to you about exploring this tradition further.
- Draw up a list of what characteristics you think a theatre tradition needs to have for you to be interested in it.

Definition: Cultural context
Cultural context relates to the factors that influence the shared beliefs, values, attitudes, products and behaviours of a society. These can include historical, geographical, political, social and technological factors.

My research into the prescribed theatre traditions

Theatre tradition	Cultural context	What it looks and sounds like in performance	What a performer has to do	What appeals and what does not appeal

What I am looking for in a theatre tradition I want to explore further as a performer

List of sources consulted

Researching the unfamiliar theatre tradition

In this section, through the activities that follow, you will be exploring the theatre tradition of Kathakali, a dance theatre tradition from India. We will be exploring this tradition very broadly. Traditions that you explore broadly and not in great depth over a sustained period can still be chosen by you for your research presentation assessment task. Getting a glimpse into the various prescribed theatre traditions throughout the course is an effective way of ensuring you get an overview of each of the traditions before you commit to your choice of tradition for the eventual task.

The cultural context and the look and feel

Research into the cultural context offers many insights into the heart and spirit of a theatre tradition. Getting a sense of a theatre tradition's cultural and social function (such as entertainment, spirituality and/or a communal sharing of stories) and the sort of performance material it uses (such as stories, issues, texts) provides you with some key information regarding how an audience is supposed to experience the theatre. It is also important to get a sense of the look and feel—or aesthetics—of the tradition so you can visualize it. Trying to research something without knowing what it is like in performance is very challenging.

Exploring Kathakali
- Read the introduction to Kathakali presented below and look at the accompanying images.

Kathakali dance theatre
By Fenella Kelly

The origins of Kathakali

Originating in Kerala in southern India, Kathakali dance theatre—literally meaning "acting out a story" (in Malayalam *katha kali* means story-play)—is a rich fusion of mime, vigorous dance patterns, acting, singing, powerful instrumental accompaniment and unique expression of emotions. It is performed by actors in highly stylized and colourful costumes, mask-like make-up and wooden crowns embellished with peacock feathers, jewels and gold leaf (Venu, 2000).

Like other traditional dance forms in India, the themes of the performances are taken from *The Ramayana, The Mahabharata* and *Bhagavata Purana*. Balakrishnan describes Kathakali as "dance, theatre, pantomime, ballet and miracle – all rolled into one, yet managing to keep its identity as a complete whole" (2004: p. 12).

Kathakali can be traced back to the middle of the 17th century and stems from the folk theatre forms of Krishnattam (stories about Krishna) and Ramanattam (stories about King Ram). The folk theatre of Krishnattam was first staged in 1657 and was created by the Zamorin of Calicut. There is a myth that states that the Raja of Kottarakkara (in northern Kerala) was hunting in the forest when he saw a performance of Krishnattam and asked the Zamorin if the troupe could come to his palace to perform (Pandeya, 1999). The Zamorin refused, and, feeling insulted, the Raja Kottarakkara Thampuram set about writing his own plays based on the story of *The Ramayana*. And so, Thampuram gave birth to Ramanattam (Balakrishnan, 2004) within ten years of Zamorin's creation. Ramanattam was later to become known as Kathakali.

Krishnattam was written in Sanskrit "the language of the gods"; Ramanattam was written in Malayalam, the "language of the people". Kathakali is mainly in Malayalam, but the *sloka* (narratives) are in Manipravalam, a mixture of Sanskrit and Malayalam (Pandeya, 1999: p. 36).

Kottayathu Thampuran wrote four plays based on *The Mahabharata* to be performed by his Kalari warriors. These performances contained choreography by the Ramanattam artist Vellat Chathu Panikkar. The Raja had a dream that the characters in the plays emerged from the sea, so the *tirasheela* (meaning wave or veil—a curtain is used) hides the characters before they are seen on stage, and they appear as if by magic. He introduced the structure of the plays and started *attakatha* (Kathakali literature). This integrated art form of *geeta* (music), *vadya* (percussion) and *nritta* (dance) was established between 1665 and 1725 (Gopalakrishnan, 2016; Venu, 2000; Balkrishnan, 2004)

Kathakali dance theatre was inspired in its performance and production elements by the martial art of kalaripayattu, the oldest theatre tradition of India, kutiyattam, and temple rituals in Kerala such as mudiyettu and theyyum. Kathakali is rooted in *The Natyasastra*, which was the first book (over 2,000 years old) to explain how to use body language to communicate with an audience. Through this form of communication, a part of the brain beyond language is used, so the beauty and clarity of body language and music can communicate a story (Sucheendran, 2020). If, when on stage, an actor performs according to the fundamental theories in this text they are transformed from a mere mortal into a graceful charmer. The most important way to achieve this sublime grace is the use of curves. In Kathakali the "actor has a large number of hand gestures to show different words [mudras] but they are not sculpted gestures: the hand follows through sinuous arcs before coming to the final stage" (Namboodiripad, 2012: p. 55). The hand is described as being "a vine curving up gracefully to show the buds that bloom from them" (ibid).

Along with *The Natyasastra*, the following temple rituals, martial arts and dance theatre traditions also informed Kathakali as we know it today.

- **Theyyum**: practised in the village temples of north Malabar. There are up to 400 different characters, each with different make-up, costumes and performance rituals. Kathakali has taken from Theyyum the ideas of make-up, headgear, pure silver ornaments and costume design. The most vigorous dance patterns in Kathakali are also adapted from Theyyam.
- **Mudiyettu**: a ritual performed in Kali temples. Elements that Kathakali took from this are: the make-up materials and designs; the stage lamp and stool; roars and other noises made by demonic characters; bloodshed; heavy costumes with exaggerated colours; the *kelikottu* (drum ensemble) to start the show and the use of the chenda drum, and *arura vadya* (percussion of the demons).
- **Kutiyattam**: India's oldest dance theatre form with the earliest records of performance dating back to 2 CE. Aspects of performance that Kathakali has imitated are: *angikam* (movement of the limbs); *vachikam* (words sung and then acted out); *aaharyam* (make-up and costume designs); *satvikam* (mental and emotional aspects, including the movement of the eyes). The *mudras* in Kathakali have been adapted from Kutiyattam.
- **Kalaripayattu**: an Indian martial art originating in Kerala. Training techniques have been taken from kalaripayattu to develop the Kathakali performers' stamina, balance, body language and fighting skills. Until recently the patrons of Kathakali were local chieftains who maintained an army, so consequently Kathakali artists were also well-trained soldiers (Balakrishnan, 2004).

The performance and performance space

Performances originally took place in the palaces of the Maharajas who had their own performance troupes, which explains the lavish gold leaf that was on the crowns, ornamental armbands, jewellery and other finery. These remain today, with many ornaments and accessories still covered in real gold. Shiva stories take place in Shiva temples, Krishna stories in Krishna temples, etc. When several stories were to be told over one or several nights, purpose-built wooden end stages were built outside a temple, so larger audiences could appreciate the spectacle (Sucheendran, 2022).

Today Kathakali is performed on a purpose-built raised platform with a roof. The acting takes place on the *arangu* (stage) and on the stage are a couple of stools and a *tirasheela* (curtain). The light for the performance comes from a large lamp (up to 1.2 m tall) filled with coconut oil. The stout burning wicks illuminate the show. For special occasions additional lamps are lit. Just behind the lamp is where the acting takes place. For some dramatic scenes, such as a chase or a fight, the actors may move amongst the audience (Venu, 2000). One or two vocalists stand upstage left. These are the *ponnani* (lead vocalist) playing the *chengilam* (gong) and the *sankiti* (assistant singer) playing the *ilattalam* (cymbals) (Balakrishan, 2004). Upstage right are the two drummers—the lead drummer plays the *chenda* (an upright drum played with sticks) and the assistant drummer plays the *madallam* (a drum played on its side, using the fingers. The fingers of the right hand are covered in *chittu*, a thimble made of cloth and a gum made of rice paste. The *madallam* is used mainly to accompany the *mudras* and the female character's dance steps.) (Gopalakrishnan, 2016).

Gopalakrishnan describes a typical Kathakali performance as follows: "it is a rare combination of pre-choreographed acting and onstage improvisations by actors, pure dance and expository dance with technically prescribed theatrics, accompanied by vivid costumes and make-up, vocal and instrumental music" (2016: p. 27).

The script and stories of Kathakali are fixed, but actors have the freedom to bring their own artistry (improvisation) to the subtleties of communication in the expression of emotion (*bhava*), feelings (*saatwika*) and the story, through the movement of the facial expressions (*navarasas*), hand gestures (*mudras*) and body movement (*aangika*), to achieve *sarvvanga bhinaya* (acting with the whole body). It takes a minimum of eight years of basic training and about a decade of experience on stage to be regarded as a Kathakali artist of some merit (ibid).

Originally 108 stories were performed but there are only about 30 now performed regularly. They are mainly based on the Hindu epics *The Ramayana* and *The Mahabharata*. The script, or *attakatha*, is vocaliszd by singers and the performers "narrate" the drama through precise movements and hand gestures. The performers play various characters, and are instantly recognizable by the colour and design of their make-up, costumes and crowns.

- **Paccha**: This category is the most beautiful and is used for royal and divine creatures, such as Lord Krishna, King Nala, princes Vishnu and Rama. The main colour used for this character is green (green symbolizes heroism and righteousness). Along the chin line is the fragile white *chutti* (an intricate mask/make-up) made of thick rice paste and paper. The paccha usually wear red jackets and white skirts.
- **Katti**: These are the anti-heroes—kings who are slaves, demonic kings and villains—such as Ravana, the evil king who abducted Sita in *The Ramayana* and Bhima, when in exile. Katti refers to the knife shape on the forehead that is painted in red and white. The katti make-up differs from the paccha by using red paint on either side of the nose bordered by a white moustache that extends to the nose. The paccha and katti wear the same crown and costume, but are opposite in temperament.
- **Tadi**: Tadi means beard. The *chuvanna tadi* (red beard), *karin tadi* (black beard) and *vella tadi* (white beard) all differ in temperament. The Hindu monkey god, Hanuman, has a white beard. Cruel characters and kings subject to darkness wear *chuvanna tadi*. The make-up is mainly red, with designs in black with white borders. Tadi wear a red furry coat, an oversized crown and an appropriately large costume. Fangs are also worn. Characters such as Kali are assigned a black beard. Monkeys wear white a furry jacket with a round headdress with silver detail.
- **Kari**: Forest dwellers and demonesses are assigned *kari* (black paint) make-up. Males are *ankari* and females are *penkari*. Black paint dominates, with other designs drawn in white and red. On the nose is a flower-like pattern made out of paper. A black beard is worn by the male character and both males and females wear

a coat and skirt of jet black. A black and white bucket-shaped headdress is worn, decorated with peacock feathers and silver. For female characters like Surpankha in *Kharavadham* and *Nakratundi* in Narakasura vhadam, there is a technique called *ninam* (blood). Some of these characters also have menacing fangs.

- **Minukku**: The face is painted yellow with a hint of red. The eyes and eyebrows are outlined with a black paste. Female characters belong to this category, as do messengers, carpenters, wrestlers and servants. Female characters cover their heads, wear special jewels and ornaments and use the sari folds for their costume. They wear artificial breasts made of wood. Servants and messengers wear regular skirts and turbans on their heads. These are gentle souls made up with subtle tones, with simple unadorned costumes.

- **Teppu**: These costumes represent many different unique performers—human beings, animals or weapons. This style of make-up is commonly used in the *Nalacaritam* story as it features lots of animals, such as swans and serpents (Venu, 2000).

In the first half of the 20th century Kathakali was dying, but it was given a new lease of life when the poet Vallathol Narayana Menon started the Kerala Kalamandalam institution in Cheruthuruthy in 1930. Training here includes dance, vocal music, instrumental music, make-up, and costumes (ibid).

Cultural role, purpose and effect on the audience

Performances tell the stories of the Hindu epics. They were and still are for entertainment, but also address morality, to show how good can overcome evil. The dramatic stories contain overarching examples of what not to do and how to live a good life.

The combination of facial expressions, body movement, footwork, *mudras*, colourful costumes, singing, drumming and percussion instruments transports the audience members to the world of the imagination and immerses them in the story. The goal of the performers is to reach the audience so that their experience is visceral—they feel the emotions of the characters, are carried along by the rhythms of the drums and the singing, and not only imagine, but also experience the story with their whole being.

The following images are all original photographs taken by Fenella Kelly (2022).

Reflection point
When looking at this collection of images, think about what additional information you get about Kathakali that you didn't get from the text. How might this inform your research into the theatre tradition? How might this inform how you present your own research to others?

Performance space

Arjuna

Bhima and Hanuman

Bhima and Panchali

Bhima killing Kichaka

Activity

Researching context and the aesthetics of the theatre tradition

- Now that you have a general idea of Kathakali, carry out some further research into any areas that you feel you need more information about, keeping a rough note of your findings somewhere handy.
- Using the information presented on the previous pages and the findings from your own research, compile rough research notes on each of the following areas using the table below/opposite to log key information and sources.

☑ **Context**—the origins and role or function the theatre tradition plays in its culture of origin

☑ **History**—its history and how it has developed over time

☑ **Performance space**—the sort of performance space traditionally used

☑ **Performance material**—the material (content) that is performed (narrative, well-known stories, play texts, sacred texts, issues, and so on)

☑ **Audience**—how audiences experience(d) the theatre tradition and what the tradition wants the audience to experience

☑ **Production elements**—what the theatre tradition looks like and sounds like (use of costumes, make-up, set, props, light, sound, and so on)

☑ **Performance elements**—who performs this and how the body and/or voice is used in performance

Findings from my research into Kathakali

Researching Kathakali	Information found (You can also include direct quotes here)	Source/evidence (Be sure to include type of source, publisher, publication date, creator or writer)
Context		
History		

Performance space		
Performance material		
Audience		
Production elements		
Performance elements		

4.3 Researching a performance convention

Now that you have an overview of the tradition it is time to research the performance conventions.

Understanding the role and use of a performance convention is a major focus for this syllabus area and for the eventual research presentation assessment task. A performance convention is a recognizable element of performance (body and/or voice) that identifies the theatre tradition. In other words, someone watching the convention would be able to identify that it belongs to a particular tradition.

You are required to pick **one** convention and research it in more depth. Each tradition has several different conventions that employ either one or a number of performance aspect(s), such as:

- face
- voice
- gesture
- posture
- movement
- manipulation of objects (e.g. puppets, props).

The performance convention we will be exploring from Kathakali is the *mudras*. The *mudras* use the performance aspects of hand gesture and face. Use the research below as an introduction to this area and then conduct further research for any areas that are unclear or that you need more information for. Try to also watch some videos that show the *mudras* in action. Remember to keep a record of your sources.

Kathakali performance convention: the *mudras*

By Fenella Kelly

The *mudras* (hand gestures)

The holistic communication of the story through bodily gestures and facial expressions is called *angikabhinaya* and is as complex as the language of speech. The entire body is used to communicate the meaning and story, but the most important aspect is the articulation of hand gestures.

"The entire concept of the language of gestures is concentrated on the palm of the hand and is embraced in its entirety in Kathakali acting.

Where the hands go, there the eyes follow;
Where the eyes go, the mind follows;
Where the mind goes, the mood (bhava) follows, and
Where the mood goes, there arises the sentiment (rasa)."
(Venu, 2000: p. 16)

The intensive training that goes into learning Kathakali is a combination of *abhinaya* (acting) and *nritya* (dancing), because the actors do not use verbal expression. Instead, the actors "speak/communicate" through mime and the use or *mudras*.

There are 24 basic hand gestures and the *Hasthalakshanadeepika* (an ancient Sanskrit text in poetry format by an unknown author) prescribes how the *mudras* are moved and combined to create words. The execution of the *mudras* takes following forms: *asamyukta mudra* (using a single hand); *samyukta mudra* (using both hands) (Balkrishnan, 2004). The *samyukta mudras* can be divided further into the following two categories: *samaanam* (the same *mudra* in both hands) and *misram* or *sankirna mudra* (different *mudras* on each hand) (Gopalakrishnan, 2016).

See a section of the *Hasthalakshanadeepika* below—first printed and published in the magazine *Kavanodayam* in 1903—that describes how to do the first *mudra* and the words that can be created.

"Pataka
Keeping the ring-finger half-bent gives rise to the Pataka hand.
The following are the double-handed usages according to Bharata: sun, king, elephant, lion, bull, crocodile … path, footstep, feet and bolt.
Single-handed usages are the following: day, going, tongue, forehead, body … and tender leaf." (Venu, 2000: p. 43)

More than 450 words can be made with the *mudras*, and not only are they done in different combinations to form the words, but also done at three different levels—waist, chest and head. Some words—for example, the *asamyukta mudra* to show the word "lady" (*katakam* done at head level) do not move from one level—but others, such as the *samaanam mudra* for "forest" (starts with *vardhamanakam*, changes to *araalam* and then to *anjali*) start at waist level move to head level and end at chest level.

When forming the words, the body and face are not static but will change to enhance the feeling or meaning of the word—the actor must employ the *navarasas* (facial expressions), to emanate the feeling of the word, and the use of their eyes and body. For example, the *samaanam mudra* for "blood" (anjali done at chest height) is accompanied by the *navarasa beebhatsam* (disgust) and the hands shimmering in a circle in front of the actor.

To learn more about how to form the *mudras* into words, search online for the following materials.
- ☑ The dictionary of Kathakali *mudras* (www.kathakalimudras.com)
- ☑ YouTube videa tutorials by Kathakali artist Kalamandala V.R. Venkitaraman (@Sahapedia and @kathakali9128)

Kathakali *mudras*
The table overleaf presents the 24 basic *mudras* in the *Hasthalakshanadeepika*—the book of hand gestures that Kathakali follows. There are *asamyukta mudras* (single hand), *samyukta mudras* (two hands doing the same thing) and *misra mudras* (two hands doing different things). They are done at three levels: head, chest and waist. Used in different combinations they can make over 450 words.

Kathakali *mudras*

1. *Patakam* (flag)	2. *Mudrakhyam* (seal)	3. *Katakam* (golden bangle)	4. *Mushti* (fist)
5. *Katharee mukham* (scissor's sharp point)	6. *Sukathundam* (parrot's beak)	7. *Kapidhakam* (apple tree)	8. *Hamsabaksham* (swan's wing)
9. *Sikharam* (mountain's peak)	10. *Hamsaasyam* (swan's beak)	11. *Anjali* (folded hands in salutation)	12. *Ardhachandram* (half moon)
13. *Mukuram* (mirror)	14. *Bhramaram* (bee)	15. *Soochimukham* (eye of a needle)	16. *Pallavam* (tender leaf, shoot)

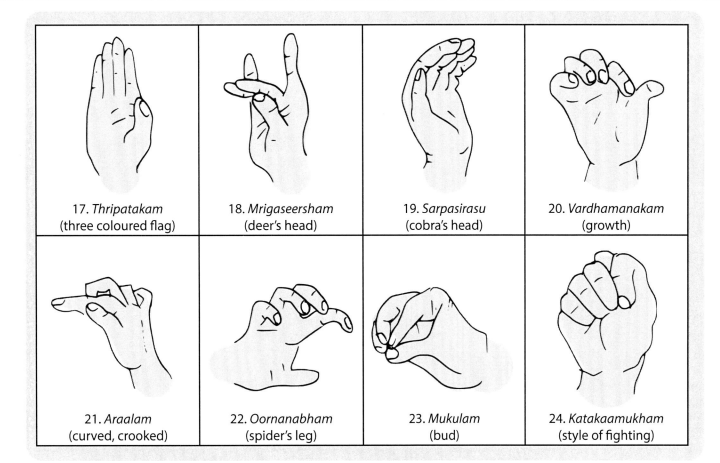

| 17. *Thripatakam* (three coloured flag) | 18. *Mrigaseersham* (deer's head) | 19. *Sarpasirasu* (cobra's head) | 20. *Vardhamanakam* (growth) |
| 21. *Araalam* (curved, crooked) | 22. *Oornanabham* (spider's leg) | 23. *Mukulam* (bud) | 24. *Katakaamukham* (style of fighting) |

Activity

Using sources and preparing a presentation

- Using the information from the previous activities, prepare and deliver a five-minute presentation with slides and a handout to introduce:
    a. the theatre tradition and its cultural context
    b. the performance convention of the *mudras*.
- Include the following three pieces of information drawn from at least two different sources.

    ☑ A quote
    ☑ An image
    ☑ A paraphrase of a piece of information from the source

- Practise presenting the information to someone else. Make sure you attribute the sources using any of the following (or any of your own) methods.

    ☑ Using a slide with the source on it in a slide show while you speak
    ☑ Referring to a handout as you speak
    ☑ Using phrases like "according to …" and "in [name of source] we find …"
    ☑ Embedding the source within your speech as a direct quote

- Prepare your presentation and film it.
- Watch it with a partner and discuss:

    ☑ if there was enough information
    ☑ the most effective and appropriate ways of attributing sources.

4.4 The practical exploration of a performance convention

Practical exploration

Practical exploration is defined by the *Theatre guide* as inquiry and research conducted through practice, using the body and/or voice to explore information, ideas, theories and/or concepts.

Practical exploration in this task is about using yourself, your own body and voice, as the main source of research. It might involve you experimenting with performance techniques, grappling with physical exercises or developing strategies in order to try out ideas or investigate what works. The purpose of practical exploration is to develop understanding through action. In many ways, your body and voice become the research laboratory where you explore performance.

In this section you will begin to plan how you will explore and develop your skills so that you can adequately embody the performance convention you have been examining. It should be understood that this task is **not** designed to train you as an expert or a performer of this convention. It takes years and years of training for someone to be qualified to be able to perform many of the conventions that you might find in a theatre tradition.

Physical warm-ups to prepare your body and voice
- Begin with a series of activities to warm up your hands, wrists and fingers. Try some of the following.

    ☑ Clench your hands into fists and then release by opening your hands with fingers outstretched. Repeat this closing and opening your hands at least eight times.

    ☑ Slowly rotate each of your wrists. Do one wrist at a time and then both wrists together.

    ☑ As you rotate the wrists make the movement bigger and bigger so that you are now moving your whole arm.

    ☑ Bend your hands down at the wrist. Slowly move them up so that they are horizontal. Then slowly move them backwards so that they are vertical, with the palms facing out.

    ☑ Put two pieces of cloth (this could be a scarf or a towel) down in front of you. Place a hand down flat on each piece. Pull your fingers up by pressing down and gathering the cloth as you bring your fingers in. Then push your fingers out flattening the cloth. Repeat this a few times.

    ☑ Extend your fingers straight out. Then bend the fingers so that your hands now look like claws. Make a fist. Then stretch the fingers out and repeat a few times.

- Now think of three new activities you would use to warm up your hands, wrists and fingers, and that might help you to prepare if you were to perform each individual *mudra*.

Activity

Activity

Trying out the convention

- Choose five different individual *mudras* from the images on pages 120-121.
- Try each one physically with your hand. Practise each one a number of times until you feel you are able to do it as accurately as you can.
- Draw a rough image of each *mudra* in the boxes below/opposite and circle any areas where you feel tension or that you have found difficult. For example, difficulty keeping your fingers together.
- Write a list of these areas of tension and difficulty. Think of activities that might help you overcome these physical difficulties.
- Repeat these activities until you feel you are now able to do each of the *mudras* you have chosen.
- Once you feel you have managed to do each *mudra* take five photographs (one of each). The photographs may show your body in its entirety or focus on a detail (for example, a photograph of just the hand/fingers).
- Prepare a five-minute demonstration, introducing and physically showing the convention and explaining how it is physically performed using the images you have captured.
- Work with a partner. Share your presentation and then "teach" each convention to your partner, leading them through a physical re-creation of the *mudra*, trying to make it as precise as possible. Capture this teaching as a video or audio recording.
- Listen to/watch your teaching of the convention and note down any further aspects that you need to introduce for the successful creation of it using the "Notes" section provided. Identify what your partner found particularly challenging about the convention and use this to guide your own future explorations.

Developing my chosen *mudras*

Mudra 1		Mudra 2	
Sketch		Sketch	
Area(s) of tension and difficulty		Area(s) of tension and difficulty	

Mudra 3	
Sketch	
Area(s) of tension and difficulty	

Mudra 4	
Sketch	
Area(s) of tension and difficulty	

Mudra 5	
Sketch	
Area(s) of tension and difficulty	

Notes

Activity

Exploring the convention

In this activity you will be exploring how you might use the convention of *mudras* to tell a story.

- Research what parts of the body are engaged when you are using *mudras*. We have focused on the hands, but find out if other parts of the body are also employed.
- Choose 3–5 *mudras* from the diagram that you think you could put together in a short story of about 30–40 seconds (or you can use the short sample story provided below).
- Make an audio recording of the story.
- Try out each *mudra*, exploring and repeating each one individually until you feel you could do them without referring to the diagram.
- Play the audio of the story and add the corresponding *mudras* to it, watching yourself in the mirror.
- Record any discoveries you make as you explore storytelling through the *mudras*.
- Now try this without the audio, with you telling the story and doing the *mudras*. Try the whole story in each of the following ways.

  - ☑ At different speeds
  - ☑ Backwards
  - ☑ In different spaces

- Once you have explored the physical nature of the performance convention, think about what physical aspects or skills you would need to develop if you were to be a performer of this convention. Think of yourself as a sports trainer or coach, and develop a programme to help you to develop the skills you might need. In this activity you will be exploring the following areas.

  - ☑ Fluidity
  - ☑ Control
  - ☑ Accuracy
  - ☑ Coordination

- Think about different practical exercises and activities to develop each of these areas. Complete the chart opposite.
- Can you think of any other elements of performance, regarding *mudras*, that need to be added to the list? Use the spaces provided to add these.
- Go through the activities and record your discoveries.

Sample story

There was once an apple tree on the peak of a mountain. This apple tree would spend each night staring at the half moon. The apple tree desperately wanted to leave the peak of the mountain in order to be together with the half moon. Its shoots would grow reaching up towards the half moon in yearning.

Practical actitvites to further develop performance elements

Performance element	Practical activity/exercise to develop this element	Discoveries
Fluidity		
Control		
Accuracy		
Coordination		

Presenting your explorations
- Once you have completed the previous activities exploring the *mudras*, make a two-minute video recording **or** a slideshow made up of images to show the different ways you practically explored the *mudras*.
- Watch the recording/slideshow of your exploration and note the key discoveries from all of the activities. Prepare a short (three-minutes maximum) podcast called "My physical explorations into the world of *mudras* from the Kathakali theatre tradition".

4.5 Experimenting with traditional performance material

In this syllabus area you are required to understand how the theatre convention you have been exploring features in an actual traditional performance. Experimenting with how the convention works in a performance gives you new understandings and insights into the theatre tradition.

A key aspect of this task is finding performance material that is traditionally performed and where the performance convention you have been exploring appears. This will give you the opportunity to experiment with the performance convention in the context of a work that it appears in.

Engaging with traditional performance material will also help you to better understand the function, role and technique of the chosen performance convention. Traditional performance material comes in different forms depending on the theatre tradition.

- Published text (this could be a description of the action)
- Published play text
- A film
- Audio
- A story
- A collection of images

The purpose of this area of the syllabus is for you to research and get a sense of how the performance convention you have been examining works in the context of a performance of that theatre tradition. This area of the syllabus and the assessment task does not require the material to be performed, but rather for it to be used as a means of experimentation. **It is important that you understand that you are not required to perform the performance material.** You must show evidence of how you use performance material to experiment.

Performance material
Below are some excerpts of traditional performance material from Kathakali dance theatre for you to experiment with.

> **Performance material 1: "The Saugandhika Flower"**
>
> "Kalyana Saugandhika" from *The Mahabharata*, by Kottayathu Tampuran
>
> (1645–1716)
>
> Scene 1: Bhima (Pandava prince) and Draupadi in the Narayana forest
> Bhima is sitting in the charming Narayana forest with his wife Draupadi. Whilst they are chatting amorously a flower drops from the sky and Draupadi picks it up. It is so beautiful, and has such an exquisite fragrance, that she asks Bhima to go on a journey to fetch her more flowers of the same sort.

Definition: Traditional performance material
Traditional performance material (written, oral, physical) is commonly performed within that theatre tradition. The performance material where the convention appears is used by the student to guide their practical exploration of, and experimentation with, the convention. Please note: the traditional performance material is intended to be chosen and used as an aid to better understanding the chosen performance convention, rather than as material that is to be performed.

Top tip
Before you undertake the research presentation task, you should first check what performance material is available for your tradition that you can access. Do this before you start your exploration process. The performance convention you choose to explore should be evident in the traditional performance material you choose. Make sure that there is enough material to provide you with opportunities for exploration and experimentation.

Verse 1 (left hand is holding the flower)

EN	KANAVAR	KANDARLUM	NEE
My	husband	see/look	you

ENGA	LORU	KOOSOOMUM
My	one	flower

This is followed by the Lady's *kalasham*.

Performance material 2: "The Killing of Kichaka"

"Keechaka Vadham" from *The Mahabharata*, by Irayimman Thampi (1782–1856)

"Keechaka Vadham", or the killing of Kichaka, in *The Mahabharata* happened during the life incognito, or the exile period, of the Pandavas who had taken refuge in the kingdom of Virata. The Pandavas assumed various roles in the palace. Panchali (Draupadi) assumed the role of a maid, named Malini, looking after queen Sudeshna and her daughter Uttara.

A powerful warrior, Kichaka, and 105 brothers known as Upakichakas also lived in Virata. Kichaka was enamoured by the beauty of Panchali and wanted to possess her. All advances of Kichaka were rejected by Panchali. Eventually Kichaka is killed by Bhima*.

Scene 3: Kichaka is in his room when Malini, the maid, (Panchali in disguise) enters with a tray of food

At the start Kichaka is looking straight ahead, then at Malini; he watches her put down the food that she has brought for him, and then looks at her lovingly. Malini ignores his advances.

Verse 3

HARINAKSHI	JANA	MOULI	MANE	NEE
Eyes like a deer	pupil	head	jewel	you

EN	ARIKIL	VARIKA	MALINI
Me	near	come	Malini

This is followed by the hero's *kalasham*.

[*Story summary adapted from Rajendran, A. (2013, May 22). *Keechaka Vadham – Story of Kichaka in the Mahabharata*. Hindu Blog. https://www.hindu-blog.com/2013/05/kichaka-vadham-story-of-kichaka-in.html]

Performance material 3: "Nala and Damayanthi"

Edited version taken from *Tales of Gods & Demons in Indian Mythology* (Shree Book Centre, 2012)

Nala, the king of Nishada, was a bachelor and sad. One day a Brahmin came to Nala's court and informed him about a beautiful princess named Damayanti. The Brahmin praised Damayanti so much that Nala fell in love with the princess, without even seeing her!

One day Nala was sitting alone in the royal garden, lost in thought. From the pools of the garden, a golden swan came up to him. "Why are you so sad, O king?" asked the swan. Nala told him about his love for Damayanti. "Can I help you in any way?" asked the swan. "Please inform her about my love for her", requested the king. So, the swan carried the king's message to Damayanti.

Soon, it returned from the princess. "She too happens to love you, O king!" said the swan. "Her father will conduct a swayamvara soon, and she will choose you as her husband." Nala was delighted to hear this.

Swayamvara—the ancient Indian tradition of choosing a husband from a number of suitors.

Performance material 4: "Ravana Vijaya"

"Ravana Vijaya" from *The Ramayana*, by Kilimanoor Raja Raja Varma Koyil Tampuran (1812–1846)

Ravana, the wicked king who conquered the whole world, behaved in a disgraceful manner. When he was in the Himalayas on his way to fight his stepbrother, Vaisravana, he saw Rhamba, a nymph who had been produced by the churning of the ocean, and was smitten with her charms.

Scene 1: Ravana and Doota
Doota (a messenger) has been sent by Vaisravana to tell his younger brother, Ravana, that he should stop his wicked ways and behave more virtuously. Ravana hears Doota's words, but makes no reply. He is so furious that he chops off the messenger's head. Ravana is determined to teach Vaisravana a lesson and is on the warpath.

Scene 2: Ravana and Rhamba
Ravana is resting on the slopes of mount Kailasa in the Himalayas. When night falls, he discovers the divine Rhamba, who is enchantingly beautiful, walking alone on her way to keep a tryst with her lover. Ravana begs Rhamba to bestow her love on him as he cannot bear to part from her.

Nymphs like Rhamba do not marry, but accept a lover for a day. Rhamba tells Ravana that she will come to him after she has spent the day with Nalakubera, Vaisravana's son, with whom she has a date. Ravana cannot wait and takes Rhamba by force. She pronounces a curse on him—the next moment he touches a woman against her will, he will die.

Performances in action
This activity builds on the previous activities exploring the *mudras*.
- Research Kathakali performances and find a filmed version of a performance or excerpts of performance(s) to watch.
- Keep a record of what is happening around the performer using the table below/overleaf.

Activity

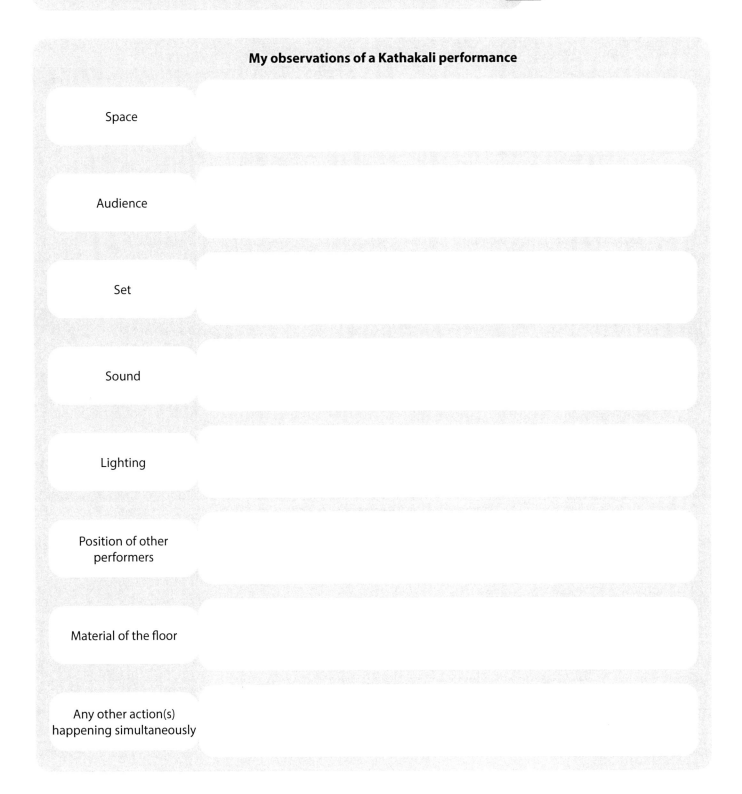

My observations of a Kathakali performance

Space	
Audience	
Set	
Sound	
Lighting	
Position of other performers	
Material of the floor	
Any other action(s) happening simultaneously	

Costume

Props

Activity

Experimenting with the convention and traditional performance material

- Look back at the performance material excerpts and choose one piece to work with.
- Identify where you think *mudras* might appear in the piece. These may be *mudras* from the illustrations provided earlier in this chapter, or you may need to do further research to find the *mudras* that correspond with the specific action of the performance material.
- Once you have identified *mudras* in the performance material, take some time to rehearse each in isolation so you feel confident doing them without referring to any images.
- Run through the *mudras* from the performance material one by one in sequence and take photographs of each.
- Caption each photograph with a line of text from the performance material.
- Research what a performer does with the rest of their body while performing a mudra.
- Experiment with how to use the rest of your body while performing the *mudras* in the performance material you have chosen. Try performing the *mudras* while also focusing on each of the parts of the body identified below.

  - ☑ Face
  - ☑ Arms
  - ☑ Chest
  - ☑ Waist
  - ☑ Legs

- Now try to bring different parts of the body together while you perform the *mudras* in the performance material.
- Reflect on how the body is used in the performance of the *mudras*.

Definition: Experimentation

This is the practical process of breaking down the chosen performance convention to determine the necessary demands and unique challenges of practically applying it to traditional performance material. The process of experimentation is about using performance material and deliberately trying out different approaches to applying the convention. This means analysing the performance material, thinking of different ways to approach the challenges of applying the convention and addressing the difficulties posed by this. Experimentation requires you to show more than one approach to how you have attempted to overcome the challenges of applying the convention to the traditional performance material.

Activity

Experimenting with applying the convention to traditional performance material

- Look back at the performance material excerpts and choose one piece to work with.
- Try to put the *mudras* into action in the performance material, using all the knowledge you have gained through research into the performances and from the previous exercises.
- Focus on how you transition from one *mudra* to another. You may also want to work on your entrance and/or exit if that is appropriate.
- Record your experiments on video or through photographs and audio.

Activity

Presenting your experiments with the performance material

- In this activity you will develop and film a five-minute presentation of your experiments. Your presentation could have a combination of you speaking, showing photographs/video of your experiments, or showing a slideshow.
- Decide on how you will best recreate and record your experiments with the performance material using the *mudras*. Only you can appear in the video. If other characters appear, use chairs or mark the floor to represent the position of their roles.
- You must include:

  ☑ an introduction to the performance material and where the section you are presenting sits within the context of the performance piece as a whole

  ☑ how you prepared for the application of the performance convention to the performance material

  ☑ a stop-and-start demonstration of the performance convention or a film you previously prepared of your experimentation with performance material.

- You can also audio record yourself speaking lines, making sounds or using recorded music that features in the performance material.
- You can also demonstrate any of the following in your presentation, which can be videoed or presented as photographs. Make sure to also include a live presentation of you demonstrating your experiments.

  ☑ Analysing the performance material and demonstrating where *mudras* appear

  ☑ Showing a warm-up you developed to help prepare you for the performance

  ☑ Showing a still image of each *mudra* in sequence

  ☑ Breaking down the performance material moment by moment

  ☑ Breaking the *mudras* down to their component parts and showing how you worked on these

  ☑ Showing how you transition and move from one *mudra* to another in the performance material

  ☑ Presenting the performance material where the convention appears as a whole and showing what needs to be worked on

  ☑ Rehearsing the *mudras* in a space comparable to the traditional space

  ☑ Rehearsing wearing clothing that might resemble what the traditional performer would wear (for example, a long skirt, something on the head to represent a crown)

- Create a storyboard of your presentation—images of what you will be doing—with text below to note what you plan to say.
- Share your presentation with your class, a partner or your teacher.

Top tip
Remember that the focus of the task is on your experiments in applying the convention to the performance material. It is not a performance.

Reflection point
Reflect on the application of a performance convention to traditional material and what approaches are best taken to make your performances authentic and respectful. You might also identify the challenges you faced in this process of application and experimentation, and how you dealt with these.

4.6 Reflecting on learning

Reflection in this syllabus area is about looking back at yourself and your learning. It requires you to identify how you think engaging with an unfamiliar theatre tradition has changed and developed:

- you as a performer
- your understanding of world theatre traditions and practices.

This gives you the opportunity to record any new perspectives or insights that you have.

It is easier to reflect if you have something concrete to reflect on, be it a journal entry you have recorded, a photograph or a video recording. That is why recording your discoveries and explorations is really important for this task. The main purpose of the next activities is, therefore, for you to look back at all the previous activities in this chapter and the recordings you have kept of your explorations into Kathakali and the *mudras*.

Developing performance skills

Teaching something to someone else is a good way to check your understanding of it.

- Imagine you will be running a practical class for younger students to help them to develop their performance skills for a production of a musical they are working on.
- Think about which performance skills can be developed for this class using some of the exercises and activities you experienced from Kathakali dance theatre and the *mudras*.
- Look back at these activities, experiments and exercises from the previous activities and plan a practical workshop of 20–30 minutes using some of the practical exercises you did or develop new activities that you think would work well to help build the musical theatre performance skills of the class.
- Using the table below/overleaf, record your workshop activities. Begin by stating which performance skills need to be targeted for the performance of a musical and identify which specific skills will be targeted by each individual activity.

Activity

My workshop plan

Performing musical theatre		
Performance skills to be developed		
Activity 1	Skill(s) to be developed	
	Description of activity	
Activity 2	Skill(s) to be developed	
	Description of activity	

Activity 3	Skill(s) to be developed	
	Description of activity	
Activity 4	Skill(s) to be developed	
	Description of activity	

Activity

Reflecting on your development as a performer
- Using the spaces provided below/opposite, explain how the practical exploration of the *mudras* from Kathakali dance theatre has contributed to your development as a performer.

My reflections on my development as a performer

Skills and understandings developed as a result of these physical activities

How these skills and understandings were developed

How, where and/or when I might use these performance skills

Understanding theatre in the world

- Looking back on your experiences of the theatre course so far, write a list of theatre traditions, practices, styles or genres you have already studied or know from previous classes.
- Using the table overleaf, compare each theatre tradition, practice, style or genre to Kathakali dance theatre, making a note of the specific similarities and differences.
- Share this with a partner and explain how your exploration of Kathakali has developed your understanding of theatre in the world.

Activity

Comparing and contrasting traditions, practices, styles and genres

Chosen theatre tradition, practice, style or genre	Similarities to Kathakali dance theatre	Differences from Kathakali dance theatre

Activity

Impact of inquiry into theatre in the world

Opposite is the IB's learner profile graphic. This highlights some of the attributes that are associated with being internationally minded and having a global perspective.

- Using the table overleaf, reflect on the learner profile attributes and consider how your exploration of a world theatre tradition developed you as a learner. What do you think were the three or four main attributes that were developed? Write notes in the space provided to explain these developments.

- Share your notes with a partner, explaining the impact of studying unfamiliar theatre traditions and practices from around the world.

IB learner profile

The aim of all IB programmes is to develop internationally minded people who, recognizing their common humanity and shared guardianship of the planet, help to create a better and more peaceful world.

As IB learners we strive to be:

INQUIRERS
We nurture our curiosity, developing skills for inquiry and research. We know how to learn independently and with others. We learn with enthusiasm and sustain our love of learning throughout life.

KNOWLEDGEABLE
We develop and use conceptual understanding, exploring knowledge across a range of disciplines. We engage with issues and ideas that have local and global significance.

THINKERS
We use critical and creative thinking skills to analyse and take responsible action on complex problems. We exercise initiative in making reasoned, ethical decisions.

COMMUNICATORS
We express ourselves confidently and creatively in more than one language and in many ways. We collaborate effectively, listening carefully to the perspectives of other individuals and groups.

PRINCIPLED
We act with integrity and honesty, with a strong sense of fairness and justice, and with respect for the dignity and rights of people everywhere. We take responsibility for our actions and their consequences.

OPEN-MINDED
We critically appreciate our own cultures and personal histories, as well as the values and traditions of others. We seek and evaluate a range of points of view, and we are willing to grow from the experience.

CARING
We show empathy, compassion and respect. We have a commitment to service, and we act to make a positive difference in the lives of others and in the world around us.

RISK-TAKERS
We approach uncertainty with forethought and determination; we work independently and cooperatively to explore new ideas and innovative strategies. We are resourceful and resilient in the face of challenges and change.

BALANCED
We understand the importance of balancing different aspects of our lives—intellectual, physical, and emotional—to achieve well-being for ourselves and others. We recognize our interdependence with other people and with the world in which we live.

REFLECTIVE
We thoughtfully consider the world and our own ideas and experience. We work to understand our strengths and weaknesses in order to support our learning and personal development.

The IB learner profile represents 10 attributes valued by IB World Schools. We believe these attributes, and others like them, can help individuals and groups become responsible members of local, national and global communities.

Reflecting on my development as a learner

Learner profile attribute developed	How my exploration of a world theatre tradition developed me as a learner in this specific area

4.7 Preparing for assessment: Structuring and recording your presentation

For the research presentation you need to submit the following.

1. A video recording of your research presentation (15 minutes maximum).
2. A list of all sources cited and any additional resources you used during the presentation (such as handouts, slideshows).

The research presentation is a 15-minute video recording. It presents your understandings and demonstrates your practical and physical explorations of a convention from an unfamiliar theatre tradition to the examiner.

Your presentation is in three parts, as follows.

Part 1: The unfamiliar theatre tradition (five minutes maximum)
In this first part, with reference to your research, you explain the unfamiliar world theatre tradition and the performance convention you have chosen to explore to the examiner. Your explanations must be supported by evidence from the primary and/or secondary sources that you have used.

Part 2: Practical exploration of the performance convention (five minutes maximum)
In this second part, you demonstrate to the examiner the process of practical exploration of the performance convention, and how you have developed an understanding of the performance convention through the body and/or voice. You will also physically demonstrate how you have experimented with applying the performance convention to traditional performance material from the world theatre tradition.

Part 3: Reflection on learning (five minutes maximum)
In this final part, you explain how your practical exploration of the performance convention has contributed to your development as a performer. You will also explain how your inquiry into your chosen theatre tradition has further developed your understanding of theatre in the world.

> **Top tip**
> The physical demonstration is not a sustained theatrical performance, but a demonstration of how you have practically explored the performance convention, broken it down, experimented with it, embodied it and applied it during your own unique process of exploration.

The video recording
Your research presentation must be captured as either:

- three discrete sections filmed over time (one for each of the assessment criteria)

or

- as one continuous take at the end of the assessment task process.

You must decide how you will capture it, in consultation with your teacher who will be able to advise what might be best for you.

The following details things to think about if you decide to record the task as three discrete sections filmed over time. Read this carefully if you decide to film in three parts as this tells you how, where, what and when to film.

What the guide says: Three discrete sections

Instructions for students completing the task as three discrete sections filmed over time
- Each section must be video recorded as **one continuous take**. Editing or adding other on-screen material to each video recorded section is not permitted.

- Each student may **rehearse and record each section numerous times** to ensure they are happy with the finished product and that the work meets the requirements of each specific criterion.
- Each student is permitted to capture sections of the presentation **in their own time** using their own recording devices or they may choose to capture certain sections in class time, using the school's recording devices. This should be negotiated with the teacher.
- The **first two sections should be recorded in a formal setting**, such as the school theatre space or classroom, while the **third section may be recorded in any appropriate setting** as determined by the student.
- It is vital that **the voice of the student is audible** throughout the entire recording. Students are advised to test their recordings to ensure that the audio is appropriately captured without distortion or distracting background noise.
- This is an individual assessment task. **Only the student being assessed may appear in the video recording** and they must be clearly visible and heard at all times.
- The **video recording device must be fixed** (either a camera on a tripod or as part of a fixed in-device camera) and **students are responsible for assembling the three video recording sections together to make one combined video file** (that does not exceed 15 minutes), which is submitted for assessment at the end of the process.

The following details things to think about if you decide to record the task as one continuous take at the end of the assessment task process. Read this carefully if you decide to film in one continuous take as this tells you how, where, what and when to film.

What the guide says: One continuous take

Instructions for students completing the task as one continuous take at the end of the assessment task process
- The research presentation must be video recorded **as one continuous take at the end of the assessment task process**. Editing or adding other on-screen material to the video recorded presentation is not permitted.
- The presentation **should be recorded in a formal setting**, such as the school theatre space or classroom.
- Each student **may rehearse and record the research presentation numerous times** to ensure they are happy with the finished product and that the work meets the requirements of each specific criterion.
- It is vital that **the voice of the student is audible** throughout the entire recording. Students are advised to test their recordings to ensure that the audio is appropriately captured without distortion or distracting background noise.
- This is an individual assessment task. **Only the student being assessed may appear in the video recording** and they must be clearly visible and heard at all times.
- The **video recording device must be fixed** (either a camera on a tripod or as part of a fixed in-device camera) and **must not be switched off at any point during the presentation**.

If you choose to film in three parts it is important that you work with your teacher to set deadlines for each part to help you with your plan and to allow your teacher to verify that you are recording each part as you are doing it.

If you choose to film as one continuous take, you must be mindful of the recommended timings and ensure that equal attention is given to each of the three assessment criteria for this task.

Use of images and other visual material

You are encouraged to show slides or visuals during your presentation if you think this will help your explanations. These need to be clearly visible in the recording as you are not permitted to add them to the video afterwards. The majority of screen time should be given to you directly addressing the lens.

All slides, images and other visual material used during the presentation must be included in the uploaded file along with the submitted list of sources.

Research presentation assessment criteria
Criterion A: The unfamiliar theatre tradition
Evidence: video recording and list of sources and resources

   i.   With specific references to their research, to what extent does the student explain the unfamiliar theatre tradition they have chosen to explore?

  ii.   With specific references to their research, to what extent does the student explain the performance convention they have chosen to explore?

What you need to do

- Choose a theatre tradition from the prescribed list and carry out primary and/or secondary research into the chosen tradition.
- Identify one performance convention from the tradition you wish to explore.
- Research the one performance convention you have selected.
- Present and video record your work in this area.

What the examiner wants to see

Criterion A(i)

- You have researched the unfamiliar theatre tradition.
- You explain what the theatre tradition is, its cultural context, and how it works.
- You use references from your research in your explanations.

Criterion A(ii)

- You have chosen and researched a performance convention from that theatre tradition.
- You explain what the performance convention is, how it works, and how it fits into the theatre tradition.
- You use references from your research in your explanations.

Research presentation assessment criteria
Criterion B: Practical exploration of the performance convention
Evidence: video recording and list of sources and resources

   i.   To what extent does the student demonstrate their process of practical exploration of the performance convention, in order to develop an understanding of the performance convention through the body and/or voice?

  ii.   To what extent does the student physically demonstrate how they have **experimented** with applying the performance convention to traditional performance material?

What you need to do

- Identify the performance aspect(s) (face, voice, gesture, posture movement and/ or manipulation of objects) you wish to employ in order to guide your practical exploration of the one convention.
- Engage in a process of practical exploration in order to develop an understanding of the performance convention through the body and/or voice.
- Identify how the performance convention is employed in traditional performance material from the tradition.
- Use performance material to further guide your practical exploration of the convention.
- Present a physical demonstration of how you experimented with applying the performance convention to the chosen performance material. This is not a performance.
- Present and video record your work in this area.

What the examiner wants to see

Criterion B(i)

- You demonstrate how you have explored the performance convention practically using your body and/or voice—it is good to actually show some of the explorations.
- You explain how you went about exploring the performance convention and how this physical exploration has given you a better understanding of the convention.

Criterion B(ii)

- You physically demonstrate how you have experimented with applying the performance convention to traditional performance material.
- You understand how the performance convention features and operates in traditional performance material.

Research presentation assessment criteria

Criterion C: Reflection on learning

Evidence: video recording and list of sources and resources

  i. To what extent does the student explain how their practical exploration of the performance convention has contributed to their continuing development as a performer?
  ii. To what extent does the student explain how their inquiry into the chosen theatre tradition has further developed their understanding of theatre in the world?

What you need to do

- Reflect on how your practical exploration of the performance convention have contributed to your development as a performer.
- Reflect on the process you have undertaken.
- Consider how your inquiry into the chosen theatre tradition has further developed your understanding of theatre in the world.
- Present and video record your work in this area.

What the examiner wants to see

Criterion C(i)

- You understand how your work on an unfamiliar theatre tradition and its performance convention has developed you as a performer.
- You identify the performance skills you have developed in this task and how they can be applied to other performances beyond the tradition you have been researching.

Criterion C(ii)

- You understand that studying one world theatre tradition opens your eyes to the bigger picture of world theatre.
- You make connections to other theatre traditions or practices that you have studied and explored on your course.

Chapter 4: Recap

In this chapter we have investigated the topic of exploring world theatre traditions, focusing on:

- researching unfamiliar world theatre traditions and their performance conventions

- approaches to practically exploring a performance convention through the body and/or voice

- practical approaches to experimenting with applying the performance convention to traditional performance material

- strategies for reflecting on your development as a performer

- ways of thinking about the development of your understanding of world theatre traditions

- how to structure your research presentation

- the requirements of the research presentation assessment task and how to prepare materials for submission to the IB.

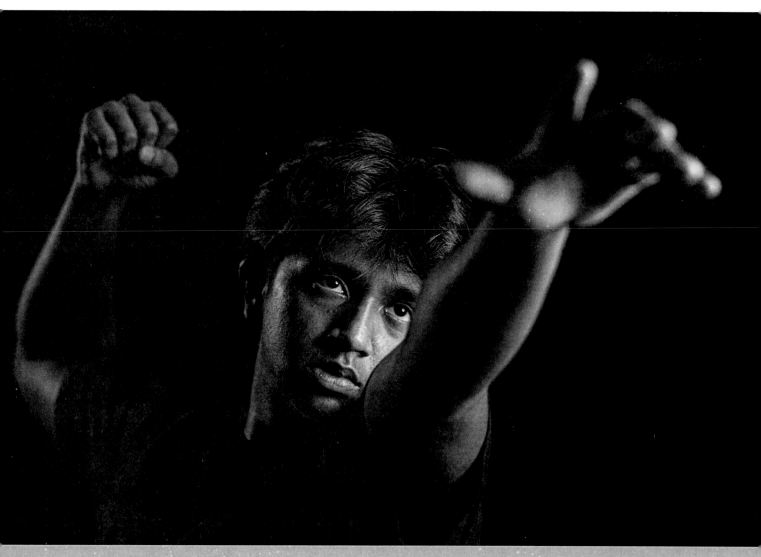

5

5. Collaboratively creating original theatre and the collaborative project

You can either work individually, in pairs or in small groups for all of the activities in this chapter.

Introduction

This chapter addresses the following areas of collaborative creation.

5.1   Building the ensemble
5.2   Choosing and exploring a starting point
5.3   Collaboratively developing theatre maker intentions
5.4   Being a creator: Devising the piece of theatre
5.5   Staging: Performing moments of tension, emotion, atmosphere and/or meaning (TEAM)
5.6   Staging: Directing, designing and production elements
5.7   Audience feedback and evaluation
5.8   Preparing for assessment: Recording the performance, writing the report and completing the cover sheet

The collaboratively creating original theatre syllabus area gives you the opportunity to work with others to create, direct, design and perform your own original piece of theatre that is 7-10 minutes in length. This piece of theatre is not based on a play text but is something unique you will create from scratch. Collaboratively creating original theatre is also known as devising and is a common way of working for many theatre companies around the world. This area of the theatre course presents an exciting opportunity to be imaginative and to work together with others to make the sort of theatre that you feel you want to make, based on material of your choice. Collaboratively creating original theatre requires you to consider what makes an effective piece of theatre as well as how to use theatre to express and communicate your ideas.

The theatre you and your **ensemble** create is based on a starting point of your choice. The *Theatre guide* provides a list of types of starting points you can choose. It is your ensemble's task to select one that you will find interesting to work with and that you feel has the most theatrical potential.

Why is this area important?
Understanding how to create, develop and stage a piece of theatre that is effective is central to this syllabus area. You can develop this understanding through studying play texts, through watching live theatre (digitally or in person) and through creating theatre and sharing it with your classmates or an external audience. Getting feedback from an audience to discover what works well and what does not is a great way of learning more about the language of theatre.

Definition: Ensemble
For assessment, you are required to work with other members of your theatre class to form an ensemble of between two and six theatre-makers. If you are the only theatre student in the class you are permitted to work with other peers that are not in your theatre class (such as theatre students from the year below, or other students who are not taking theatre), as long as the ensemble size does not exceed six people.

Play, curiosity, experimentation and risk-taking are all essential features of successful collaborative creation. The joy of making original theatre is that it is open-ended and the result, though guided by an intention, is often completely unknown. Embracing this uncertainty and the unknown will help you to approach this endeavour with confidence and playfulness. It encourages you to be open-minded, imaginative and a problem-solver as there will inevitably be challenges that need resolving, material that does not work and ideas that do not go anywhere.

Creating an original piece of theatre

The *Theatre guide* provides a project brief to help steer the development of the final theatre piece. This brief is designed to help shape your approach to theatre-making and to make the experience of creating the piece more authentic.

> **Project brief**
> Imagine your ensemble is a small, collaborative, low-budget touring theatre company that is required to create a piece of theatre (7–10 minutes maximum) that could feasibly tour. Working in this way will mean that you do not need to make your production too complex and that you do not add too many unnecessary layers to your work in terms of production elements (scenic and technical).

The collaborative project assessment task requires you to take on the multiple perspectives of **creator**, **director**, **designer** and/or **performer**. At some point you will need to consider all these perspectives when you are making and staging the piece. It is also essential to ensure that your ensemble creates enough theatrical material to allow for everyone in the group to be individually assessed— the examiners want to see each individual ensemble member's performance skills and their specific individual artistic contributions as creator, designer and/or director.

The specific requirements of the collaborative project assessment task are as follows.

What the guide says
For the collaborative project assessment task each student in the ensemble is required to submit the following.
- A completed cover sheet
- A video recording (7-10 minutes maximum) of the final piece
- An individual project report (10 pages of written text and images, with written text not exceeding 4,000 words maximum) that is a written account of your involvement in the collaborative project.
- A list of any sources used (these are not included in the word count)
- The project report is assessed on-screen. You must ensure that your work is clear and legible when presented in a digital, on-screen format. The work should be created using a common page size (A4 or US Letter), be typed in a legible sans serif 12-point font and use standard margin sizes and single spacing. The project report may also contain legible handwriting.

To achieve this, the collaborative project task requires you to undertake the following process.

- Form an ensemble of 2–6 students from the theatre class. This will be your group for the entire process of this assessment task.
- Offer a starting point to the ensemble and explore this theatrically.
- As an ensemble, collaboratively decide and develop overall intentions, structure and content for the theatre piece.

- Create a piece of original theatre that is developed from the chosen starting point and fulfils your ensemble's intentions. You will need to contribute to the development and staging of this piece as creator, designer and/or director so you can be assessed on how effective your specific artistic contributions were in achieving the ensemble's intentions.
- Prepare the final piece for an audience as a fully realized production. This will involve making decisions regarding the production elements as well as rehearsing the piece to ensure it is polished and ready for sharing with a live audience.
- Perform in the final piece to an audience (the performance must last between 7 and 10 minutes) and capture a video recording of the live performance. You will be assessed on how you have used your performance skills to create a moment of tension, emotion, atmosphere and/or meaning ("TEAM") in the performance.
- Capture audience feedback which will be used by you for your own evaluation.
- After the performance is over, take some time to watch back the video recording of the piece. Choose the following for assessment:

  ☑ **One** moment from the video recording (two minutes maximum) to evidence your most effective performance skills.

  ☑ **One** moment from the video recording (two minutes maximum) to evidence your best artistic contributions to the development and/or staging of the piece as creator, designer and/or director. **This moment must be different to the one you chose to use as evidence of your performance skills.**

- Complete the cover sheet provided by the IB and submit your work.

The culture of collaboration

Working as part of an ensemble develops your collaborative skills and encourages you to negotiate, listen and solve problems as part of a group. These are lifelong skills that go beyond theatrical practice. The culture of collaboration should be built on mutual respect, listening to each other, valuing other people's suggestions and ideas, and creating a safe space for contributing and sharing ideas. This spirit of "ensemble" should underpin your work in all syllabus areas. However, in this syllabus area more than others, it is vital to work with mutual respect, responsibility, and collaboration.

For this area of the course you need to be conscious of how an ensemble works and a consciousness of your own actions and how they affect others. You also need to be aware of how other people work best to find ways to inspire and energize and support them, even when you disagree with their ideas. The best way of achieving this is to constantly reflect on your actions, to consider your own preferred methods of working, to recognize what inspires and energizes you, and to identify the situations and process that you find challenging. As a result of this awareness, you will be in a better position to be a positive and supportive collaborator.

Assessment criteria

The collaborative project is assessed using the following criteria.

	Collaborative project	Marks	Total
A	The collaborative creative process and performance	8	
B	Individual contributions to the performance	8	24
C	Effectiveness of individual contributions seen in the video recording	8	

The activities outlined in this chapter have been designed to fully prepare you for success in each of these areas.

Top tip

The *Theatre guide* provides specific criteria for assessing your performance skills and for assessing your individual artistic contributions to the piece. These criteria are discussed in depth later in this chapter. Being familiar with these requirements before you begin the process of creating the piece will ensure that you know exactly what is required of you at every stage in the project.

Reflection Point

How easy do you find collaboration? What do you enjoy about it? What do you find challenging? What worries you about this syllabus area? What excites you?

5.1 Building the ensemble

Theatre is a collaborative art form. As such, it's important to think about ways of creating a healthy group dynamic and a culture of collaboration that encourages contributions from everyone and where everyone feels valued.

Being a good collaborator helps to establish a strong and positive working environment. It is important for every member of the group to feel able to honestly offer feedback and to challenge ideas, so that decisions can be made collectively and so that the most appropriate and effective choices are made regarding the final piece of theatre.

If members of your ensemble feel unable to speak out or to offer a challenge with new ideas, you can see this as an indicator that the ensemble is not a safe space for collaboration. No matter how well you may know each other or how many times you may have worked together before, whenever you find yourself in a new group or starting a new project, you will need to "reset". Working with other people will always generate different dynamics and different ways of working. For this reason, every group has to begin by actively and consciously transforming itself from a group of individuals into an ensemble at the start of every new project or piece of collaborative work. This means deliberately paying attention to the different individuals in the group, listening to their needs, and identifying agreed ways of working to establish the conditions that will best lead to the most effective theatrical collaboration and end results.

The following activities are specifically designed to help establish this ensemble approach and to effectively build trust.

Activity

Defining ensemble
- Using the space below, write a list of the ingredients that you believe help create a culture of collaboration.
- In the space provided opposite, draw a picture or diagram that visually communicates how an effective ensemble works. Alternatively, you may wish to capture photographs to illustrate this.
- In the final box, write a profile of characteristics and attitudes that make up an effective collaborator in a theatre ensemble. This is about the nature of each individual their approaches and behaviours. You might also want to use the IB learner profile as inspiration.

Building a collaborative ensemble

Ingredients for a culture of collaboration

The effective ensemble

Characteristics and attitudes that make up an effective collaborator in a theatre ensemble

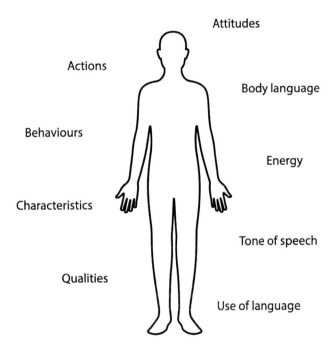

Attitudes

Actions

Body language

Behaviours

Energy

Characteristics

Tone of speech

Qualities

Use of language

Reflection, evaluation and collaboratively creating original theatre

Reflection is a key part of collaboratively creating original theatre. When working in an ensemble it is important to be aware of your own actions, words, and attitudes. Awareness means that you can consciously work to ensure that your ensemble is creatively productive, efficient, and collaborative. It means that you can purposefully track your own actions and contributions—charting the process of developing yourself and your piece of theatre.

There are different areas that you need to think about and evaluate as you work on this syllabus area and assessment task. Your reflections and your continuous evaluations will help you to decide on what action needs to be taken and what happens next. These focal points are illustrated below.

Areas for consideration

The following activities build on these areas and offer a place to begin to chart your development as a creative collaborator.

Activity

The ensemble and I
- Complete an audit of how you work with other people by completing each statement.

My reflections on myself as a collaborator

I feel challenged when...

When I feel challenged I...

I work best when others...

I feel confident when...

I feel most inspired when...

When my ideas
are not used I…

The best thing
about working in
an ensemble is…

I'm triggered
when someone…

When we work with others, we often adopt a particular role that we feel most comfortable with. This sometimes also depends on the situation.

- Take a look at the four collaborator roles identified below and consider the following.

    ☑ Which of the following roles do you enjoy the most?
    ☑ How do you demonstrate this role through what you say and do?

- Use the spaces below to capture your responses.

Initiator: "I like to come up with ideas and to help inspire others"
Supporter: "I support and encourage others and prefer to work with others to develop their ideas"
Peacekeeper: "I try to ensure that everyone works well together and I focus on resolving conflict"
Problem-solver: "I like to use my imagination and creativity to solve problems"

The role I enjoy the most

The ways in which I demonstrate this role

Activity

Contracting

Contracting is the process where agreements are negotiated and approved by the different members of the ensemble. Sometimes these agreements are already implicitly understood and demonstrated, especially if you are working with people you already know well. In other situations, these need to be explicitly drawn up by the group. These can sometimes be known as ground rules, a manifesto for collaboration or as shared agreements.

- Working individually or in a group write the following in the space provided below.

  ☑ A list of guidelines for collaboration for the ensemble

  ☑ A list of the group's expectations and some ground rules for behaviours

  ☑ A list of agreed strategies to be employed when a challenge or problem arises (for example, "I don't feel listened to" might be addressed by "Let's all listen without interruption" or "I am doing all the work" might be addressed by "Let's each take on a specific task")

The collaboration charter

Our guidelines for collaboration

Our expectations and ground rules for our behaviours

Strategies we can use when we face challenges

There are a wide variety of different practical activities and exercises that can be effectively used to develop ensemble and strengthen group work. Here are a few examples.

Categories of activities for building an ensemble	
Breathing exercises	Reflection activities
Challenges and overcoming obstacle games	Rhythmic exercises
Concentration exercises	Silly games
Discussion-based activities	Silent communication activities
High-energy activities	Still exercises
Imaginative exploration and visualization exercises	Storytelling exercises
Improvisation	Tag-based games
Relaxation exercises	Team competitive games
Physical contact exercises	Trust exercises
Problem-solving activities	Vocal and sound exercises
Repetition exercises	Word games

The next activity builds on these categories and will help you identify some of the group exercises and activities you already know, and to also help you create your own new ones.

Activity

Building ensemble

- Look at the categories of activities for building an ensemble on the previous page. Choose the five of these categories that you find most effective for ensemble building.
- Using the space provided below, compile a list of any games/activities you already know from each of the categories that you selected.
- Imagine the titles below are the names of ensemble-building activities. Choose three titles and make up your own exercises or games that can be carried out with a group for ensemble building. Each game/exercise must develop particular aspects of an ensemble. Have a go at running one or all of these with your group.

☑ All aboard
☑ All for one and one for all
☑ Catch me I'm falling
☑ Connecting flights, avoiding fights
☑ Get out of here
☑ I to I
☑ Interweave
☑ Over the mountain, over the moon
☑ Rhythm of the group
☑ We carry us

	Ensemble-building exercises	
	Chosen category	*Linked games/activities to help strengthen collaboration*
1		
2		
3		
4		
5		

Professional companies that collaboratively create original theatre

Inquiring into the work of professional theatre companies that collaboratively create original theatre can provide you with models of collaborative creation as well as resources, activities and ideas that you can use as inspiration in your own theatre making. Some theatre companies also provide free online materials and resources that share the types of exercises they use to develop ensemble and to create original theatre.

The following activity gives you the opportunity to find out more about a specific theatre company and enables you to engage more directly with their process of collaborative creation.

> **Top tip**
> Make sure you always attribute any source that has inspired you or given you specific ideas for your theatre work, even if this has come from the work of a professional theatre company.

Researching a company that collaboratively creates original theatre

- Research theatre companies that collaboratively create original theatre. Be sure to look at both companies that are based in the country you live in and internationally.
- Choose one company that you like the look of and carry out research into the areas listed below. Record your findings in the space provided below/ overleaf.

  - ☑ The company's intentions
  - ☑ Their approaches to creating original theatre
  - ☑ The look and feel of the company's productions
  - ☑ Any exercises or activities the company uses to create original theatre

- Draw a diagram to broadly illustrate the process the company follows to create original theatre. Share your diagram and findings with a partner.

Activity

Exploring the work of a collaborative theatre company

Chosen theatre company	
The intentions of the company	

Their approach to creating original work

The look and feel of their theatre productions

Exercises or approaches they use to create original theatre work

The process the company follows to create original theatre work

5.2 Choosing and exploring a starting point

The *Theatre guide* provides a list of categories of starting points that your ensemble is required to choose for the collaborative project assessment task. It is important to choose carefully as the starting point should be inspiring and rich with theatrical possibilities. It should excite you all, ignite your imaginations and be something you feel allows the group to explore their interests and make the sort of the theatre you want to make and that you believe in.

What the guide says

The starting point provides the inspiration for the collaborative creation of the piece of theatre. It gives a focus to the initial stages of practical exploration. For this assessment task, the starting point must be one of the following:

- an event
- an idea, issue, question or theme
- an image or photograph
- a non-dramatic text
- an object
- a person
- a piece of music
- a site (place/location)
- a piece of street art, a graphic novel or a comic strip.

The guide goes on to explain that the starting point is like the launch pad for your ideas. As such, your final piece of theatre may not resemble the starting point in any way at all—it is just the initial ignition to get the creative process started. The exploration of the starting point will in turn lead to the creation of the collaborative theatre-making intentions that will then become the way you monitor the effectiveness of your final piece.

"As theatrical material is drawn out of the starting point and practically explored and developed, the focus and subject matter of the piece will become clearer to the ensemble and they will discover the areas of interest that yield the most possibilities. As a result of this development, the subject matter of the final piece may move away from the initial point considerably. It may be useful for students to record the process of evolution of the theatre piece from starting point to final production as a reminder to help them at a later stage with their reflection on collaboration." (*Theatre guide*)

Top tip
Try to avoid spending a lot of time discussing and deliberating the possibilities, implications and effectiveness of a starting point. The best way is to test the starting point by working practically as quickly as possible to prevent valuable time getting lost through inaction. This way you can try out ideas and see if they excite you.

Here is an example of how a starting point could potentially develop into a piece of theatre.

- ➤ Your ensemble chooses the starting point of a photograph of children playing in a playground.
- ➤ Your group explores this and experiments with ideas. Your group decides that the final piece will be about old age and will be performed in a residential care home.
- ➤ The final piece will focus on the hopes and dreams of the elderly and will not actually consider childhood at all.

As you can see, there are an endless number of possible directions a theatre piece can go in, and your chosen starting point is just the beginning. And hopefully the more powerfully rich, provocative, and exciting the chosen starting point is, the more original, engaging and meaningful the final piece will be.

Making a choice
There are many different processes by which a starting point may be chosen. Each person can bring in a starting point of their choice and the ensemble discusses each of these and chooses one they want to work with. Alternatively, the ensemble might decide together on a particular area they want their theatre piece to be about and they then collectively choose a starting point. Regardless of the process chosen, it is important to begin by creating some criteria to help you assess the suitability and effectiveness of any potential starting point. The following activity will help you to establish some basic principles.

Example starting points		
1	An event	The first landing on the moon
2	An idea, issue, question or theme	Conspiracy theories

3	An image or photograph	
4	A non-dramatic text	"To walk in someone's footsteps is an act of commemoration and an act of empathy. It indicates undertaking a journey that has already been made by someone else at some other time. To place your feet within another's footprints suggests a desire to experience the world as the other has experienced it, to see the world as they have seen it. In this respect, it is a desire to see the world through the lens of someone else's memories. Memory can provide the map and the means, the transport, that can take you on such a journey into someone else's past. To walk in a parent's footsteps can also indicate a journey into the landscape that we call heritage, on a journey that is part of a family legacy." **An excerpt from an anonymous essay on memory**
5	An object	A box of matches
6	A person	Rosa Parks (b.1913)
7	A piece of music	A national anthem
8	A site (/location)	The resting place of the dead
9	A piece of street art, a graphic novel or comic strip	

Effective starting points

Take a look at the list of example starting points provided opposite.

- Using the space provided below, put the examples of starting points in order of how effective you think they are for the creation of an original piece of theatre. Put what you think is the most effective first and the least effective last.
- Provide a rationale to explain why you have put them in that order and write a list of qualities that you think a starting point should have based on your top choices.
- Look through the rationales you have provided. These insights can now be used as a checklist to help you select an effective starting point you would like to work with.

What makes a starting point effective?

Example starting point	Rationale for my choice

Exploring a starting point

With a partner or in a small group, choose one starting point to work on. This can be any of the ones already listed or one of your own choosing. **This starting point will be used in all the following activities, which are designed to take you through a process that will prepare you for the real assessment task.**

When choosing a starting point, it is important to ensure that everyone in the ensemble is happy with the choice and is committed to working with it. The following checklist can help the group to decide if everyone is happy with the starting point that has been put forward.

> **Is it a starting point that you are all interested in and that you would like to bring to life?**
> This should be something that inspires you all individually and that you think will inspire the sort of theatre you want to make.

> **Is it a starting point that deals with interesting ideas?**
> You need to find a starting point that deals with ideas, themes, or issues the ensemble is interested in exploring.

> **Is it a starting point that has creative possibilities for performers?**
> You need to choose a starting point that gives the ensemble the chance to be creative. It must also be one that offers possibilities for performance and for each member of the ensemble to have a substantial performance opportunity.

> **Is it a starting point that has exciting possibilities for design and for the use of production elements?**
> When choosing a starting point, you should also consider it from a theatre design point of view. This involves visualizing and thinking about what sort of space the final piece might be performed in and what set, lights, costumes, sound, and props you might want to utilize to bring it to life.

> **Is it starting point that has interesting moments of action or can be turned into an interesting story?**
> When you explore the starting point you should be able to identify key moments of action or a story that you think would be exciting to stage.

Once you and your group are entirely happy with the chosen starting point it is time to start exploring it. The following activities are designed to lead your ensemble through the process of exploration. Try to keep a record of all your explorations as they may well offer potential material for your final piece of theatre.

The ideas in the starting point

Each starting point will contain lots of ideas and themes that could become the focus of your piece of theatre.

- Take a table and two chairs. Using any materials you have at hand or that you can source, create an **installation**—a sort of physical sculpture or exhibit—that represents all the possible ideas of the starting point that you've chosen.
- Use cards, sticky notes or pieces of paper to write down text, words and quotes that emerge from the starting point, as well as drawing sketches or sourcing images. Use these almost like footnotes and position them in relation to your objects to make this an installation of all possible ideas.
- Once the installation or sculpture is complete you can also position people in it.
- Take a photograph and use this image to identify the most striking themes and ideas contained in the starting point. Make a note of these in the space provided below. These can be used as a guide for the practical explorations.

Ideas from chosen starting point

Chosen starting point	
Striking themes and ideas contained in the starting point	

There are countless ways to explore a starting point. The diagram below captures some of the most effective approaches to active exploration along with some specific examples of possible exploration activities.

Type of exploration	Example
Games and exercises	Work with the ensemble to explore how to transform a game of chase/tag into a movement sequence about bullying.
Visual	Work with the ensemble to draw images of different emotional states on a piece of paper that are then transformed into face masks to explore identity.
Physical	Work with the ensemble to explore how to show a refugee parent and child's journey over a dangerous terrain using just bodies and chairs.
Voice-led	Work with the ensemble to tell the story of *Beauty and the Beast* using only voice-made sound effects.
Written	Work with the ensemble to write monologues based on characters in paintings by Edward Hopper.
Spatial	Work with the ensemble to transform the theatre space into different rooms in an apartment building and explore the different people who live in each of them.
Playing with materials	Work with the ensemble using various lengths of rope, bedsheets and a ladder to explore a play set on a haunted ship.
Playing with production elements	Work with the ensemble to set up a single follow spot and use sound effects of political speeches or military music to explore the idea of disappearances and human rights violations in totalitarian regimes.

The following activity builds on this exploration and encourages you to begin working with your ideas practically.

Strategies for exploring the starting point

- Look at the guide to explorations diagram and the examples provided opposite as possible approaches to exploring a starting point.
- Select three types of exploration and try them with your group, using the specific examples provided.
- Next, adapt these three approaches to explore your chosen starting point and any themes or ideas related to it that you identified from your installation in the previous activity.
- Capture photographs of a moment from each of the three explorations and share these with the group.

Activity

Setting goals

- Reflect on what you discovered regarding the starting point as a result of the practical explorations you have conducted by completing each of the sentences in the goal setting section below. Share these with your partner or other members of your group.
- Use your findings from the reflection to decide what you want your final piece to be about, the **performance style(s)** you want to create your piece in, and the effect it will have on an audience.

Activity

Definition: Performance style

Performance style relates to how a piece of theatre is presented on stage. Naturalism is an example of one such theatre styles and utilizes traditionally established conventions of theatre to create a sense of realism. Another example is surrealism, which is characterized by the use of unexpected, illogical or dream-like theatrical devices and effects.

Reflection and goal-setting

As a result of this exploration, I have discovered:

I would like to further explore:

I think it would be interesting if we created a piece of theatre inspired by this starting point about/ that:

5.3 Collaboratively developing theatre-maker intentions

The collaborative project assessment task requires you to write a collaborative statement of theatre-maker intentions. This is the statement of the ensemble's vision and is key in helping your ensemble to keep its final destination in sight. Your theatre-maker intentions keep you on track, as well as providing you with a concrete benchmark against which you can evaluate your final piece at the end of the project.

The *Theatre guide* explains what the collaborative theatre-maker intentions should include.

What the guide says

Theatre-maker intentions
Students are required to collaboratively formulate intentions for the piece of theatre (200 words maximum). These must be agreed by the ensemble and should include the following.
- The chosen starting point
- What the piece will address or explore
- The target audience for the piece
- The performance space and the positioning of the audience
- The effect the ensemble aims to have on their target audience

Ethical theatre-making
You need to ensure that you make ethical and responsible choices in your work when it comes to the use of ideas or language that could be deemed offensive, inappropriate or inflammatory.

Your work must not:
- damage the environment
- express ideas or use language that incites or condones prejudice or discrimination
- glamorize the taking of illegal drugs
- inappropriately reference socially taboo subjects
- incite or condone intolerance or hatred of others
- include excessive or gratuitous violence
- make reference to, or represent, explicit sexual activity.

The ensemble needs to construct one collective statement of intention. This will be the same statement that is used by all members of the group on their individual cover sheet that tells the examiner what the theatre-maker intentions for the group are.

As mentioned previously, having clear intentions means that you have thought about what material you want to explore, what you want to say, how you want to say it and what effect you want it to have on the audience. This means that your theatre-making is responsible and that it has considered both purpose and impact. The IB also provides some guidance regarding the type of content that you choose and making ethical theatre-making decisions. You should consider this when you are developing both your intentions and your piece of theatre.

The process of putting together the collaborative theatre-maker intentions should, to an extent, be an editing process where different ensemble members' contributions are combined into one coherent aim. In order to guide a group's work, the statement needs to be clear and everyone needs to understand what it is saying and the implications regarding the piece of theatre that is going to be made. Make sure you are happy with the statement before you begin your work.

Writing your intentions

- Working with your partner or in your small group, but without others seeing what you are doing, write your own individual proposed intentions for the theatre piece in section one below/overleaf. Try to limit the response in each box to no more than 20 words.
- Once you have completed this, come together with the ensemble or your partner and invite each person to explain their ideas regarding the intentions they have written. No one should ask questions or comment until everyone has had their turn sharing.
- Once everyone has shared their ideas, take some time to discuss the ideas that have been explored. As a group, collaboratively negotiate what the aims of the piece will be in light of all of the contributions. Write these agreed responses in the second section provided overleaf.
- Come together as an ensemble/pair and share your drafts.
- Next, using a whiteboard or large piece of paper, draft a 200-word statement that captures all of these agreed elements. The statement must not exceed the word limit, so take some time to ensure it is precise and that it appropriately reflects the agreements of the group. Once you have this drafted, write it up in the third section provided overleaf. This statement captures your guiding theatre-maker intentions for the next stage of your work.

Activity

Top tip
As you start to develop your theatre piece, you may make new discoveries that change the nature of your work. Your theatre-maker intentions can always be slightly altered and modified as you go through the process of development, but they should not veer too far away from your initial version. If you change your overarching intentions too much during the process of creation it may take you off-course and possibly make all the work you have done so far redundant.

Section 1: My proposed intentions

Description of the starting point

What the piece will address or explore (ideas, themes)

Story (if applicable)

Target audience

The effect the piece should have on the target audience

The performance space and positioning of the audience

Section 2: The ensemble's collaboratively agreed intentions

Description of the starting point

What the piece will address or explore (ideas, themes)

Story (if applicable)

Target audience

The effect the piece should have on the target audience

The performance space and positioning of the audience

Section 3: Our agreed statement of intentions (200 words maximum)

5.4 Being a creator: Devising the piece of theatre

The collaborative project assessment task differentiates between the **creation and development of the piece of theatre** and its **staging**.

The **creation** and **development** of a theatre piece

The **staging** of a theatre piece

After all, something that does not exist cannot be staged. Although in some instances these processes might overlap, the first part of the process is to **create** and **develop** material for the piece of theatre without worrying how polished or ready it is for an audience; otherwise, you could end up spending all your time perfecting the first scene for an audience and never moving beyond it.

The second part of the process is **staging** the piece. Staging is defined in the guide as the proposed choice and use of performance and production elements in a performance space to fulfil stated theatre-maker intentions. This part of the process is usually called rehearsal and this involves getting the piece ready for an audience. This involves direction and design, and the introduction and preparation of the production elements that contribute to effective staging.

Before you begin making your theatre piece it is important to have an idea of a process for the creation, development and staging. Understanding what the process entails and knowing the different strands of this process will help everyone in the ensemble stay on track and work collectively at the same pace. It provides you with a road map for the process, prepares you for the various milestones you need to reach and helps you organize your time.

The following are some different models that can be used for the creation, development and staging of original theatre.

Model 1
Collective creating, developing and staging of an original piece of theatre
Everyone in the ensemble works on the creation, development and staging of the piece of theatre as a whole. No one is assigned any particular area of theatre-making (performer, designer, director) at any time. Decisions about all aspects of creating, developing and staging are always made as an ensemble.

Process of creating and developing the piece
The ensemble collectively creates and develops the piece.

Process of staging the piece
The ensemble collectively stages the piece, preparing it for an audience, with everyone performing, directing and designing.

Model 2
Assigned roles for creating, developing and staging of an original piece of theatre
Everyone in the ensemble is assigned a particular theatre-maker role from the beginning and given responsibility for that area. The ensemble works together on the creation, development and staging of the piece of theatre, but each individual looks at the piece from the perspective of their own particular theatre-maker role. Everyone is required to perform in the piece.

Process of creating and developing the piece
The ensemble collectively creates and develops the piece, but each person contributes to the creation and development of the piece from the perspective of their theatre-making role. Everyone is also required to perform in the piece.

Process of staging the piece
Particular individuals are responsible for the design and direction of the piece. Design and direction responsibilities can be specialized. For example, one individual may be in charge of the design of costumes, while another is in charge of the lighting design; one individual may be in charge of directing physical work, whereas another is responsible for directing musical scenes.

Model 3
Collective creating and developing followed by assigned roles for the staging of an original piece of theatre
Everyone in the ensemble works on the creation and development of the piece. Once the piece has been created individuals then take a directing or design responsibility for the staging of the piece.
Process of creating and developing the piece
The ensemble collectively creates and develops the piece.
Process of staging the piece
Particular individuals are responsible for the design and direction of the piece. Design and direction responsibilities can be specialized. For example, one individual may be in charge of the design of costumes, while another is in charge of the lighting design; one individual may be in charge of directing physical work, whereas another is responsible for directing musical scenes. Everyone is required to perform in the piece.

Reflection point
Which model most appeals to you and why? Discuss these models with your partner/ensemble and decide which you will adopt or develop one of your own.

Model 4
Shifting roles for the creation, development and staging of an original piece of theatre
Everyone in the ensemble works on the creation, development and staging of the piece and adopts various directing or design responsibilities for the staging of the piece as they are required.
Process of creating and developing the piece
The ensemble collectively creates and develops the piece.
Process of staging the piece
Particular individuals take responsibility for the design and direction of the piece as required. For example, one individual, as well as performing, may be the director of one scene, the designer of the costumes for another scene and the music director for another.

The role of the creator

Being a creator is a bit like being a playwright. Although the collaborative project task does not require a dedicated writer, members of the ensemble do need to find ways of capturing and recording the piece as it develops. It is very easy to forget what you have created when you are working practically and it is important to keep a record of each scene that has been created so you can then review them and decide what to keep, what to lose and what order the material should be in.

It is possible to keep a record of the development of the piece in the following ways.

- Video-recording scenes.
- Writing a description of the scenes
- Writing a script
- Photographing key moments
- Creating a **storyboard**

Being a creator in the collaborative project can involve the following actions.

- ➢ Having an idea related to the theatre-maker intentions and working with the ensemble to bring it life.
- ➢ Offering inspirations to the group that can be used to create a scene.
- ➢ Shaping the content of a scene or a moment to see what it is like in action.
- ➢ Writing dialogue for a scene or for a character.
- ➢ Experimenting with production elements.
- ➢ Bringing in material (text, images, music, sound, props, materials) related to the starting point that can be used as a prompt for the development of a scene.
- ➢ Directing a moment of action that has not yet been created.
- ➢ Leading a game or activity that can then be turned into theatrical material.
- ➢ Offering a performance that you have prepared to the group.

The following activity puts you in the role of creator and takes you through the steps of creating theatrical material that you can continue to develop for the remainder of this section (5.4).

Activity

Creating scenes
- Look at the starting point the group has chosen and the collaborative theatre-maker intentions you developed in the previous activities.
- With your partner or small group, create four short scenes based on the starting point and intentions that are no more than two minutes in length. The scenes should be created using the following guidelines.
  - ➢ One scene is a movement or physical theatre piece and must include music or sound effects.
  - ➢ One scene is a **naturalistic** scene with only five lines of dialogue.
  - ➢ One scene is a series of monologues that each take place in a different location.
  - ➢ One scene uses a narrator or storyteller.
- Record each scene using any method (such as video, written text or photographs).
- Give each scene a title and write this in the space provided overleaf.

Definition: Naturalism
Naturalistic theatre aims to create the illusion of real life on stage, with the actors seemingly unaware of the audience watching them.

Scene titles	
Scene 1	
Scene 2	
Scene 3	
Scene 4	

Developing material and problem-solving

Once you have created your scenes, you may want to revisit them to develop them further. Often, giving yourself a constraint or a key ingredient that you must include in a scene can provide you with different perspectives as well as inspiring a more imaginative approach.

Artistic constraints or limitations are useful as ways to encourage creativity. Working in an open-ended way where anything can happen is often more challenging for creativity. These given constraints, conditions or new perspectives may offer a very useful approach to problem-solving.

The following activity offers some creative constraints to challenge you. See how you can creatively overcome what might at first seem like a limitation.

Reflection point
How did you respond to working with the creative approaches, limitations and constraints? Did anything surprise you? What was the most effective moment you created? How might you employ this technique in the future?

Different approaches

- Apply one or more of the following approaches to one of the scenes that you have created in the previous exercise. This will give you a different perspective on the scene and allow you to reshape it, give it more depth or make it more theatrically effective.

Activity

- ☑ Make the space bigger
- ☑ Make the space smaller
- ☑ Recreate the scene imagining that the audience is watching from above
- ☑ Use one chair
- ☑ Change the style
- ☑ Introduce a character who never speaks
- ☑ Change the setting
- ☑ Add a flashback
- ☑ Add a moment of direct address to audience
- ☑ Make an object the focus of the scene
- ☑ Add a costume change on stage in the middle of the scene
- ☑ Have a performer change character in the middle of the scene
- ☑ Involve the audience

Structuring the piece

Structure is key when creating original theatre. The positioning of scenes is a key part of the development of your piece of theatre. The positioning of one moment alongside another is also one of the key ingredients in communicating the messages of a piece of theatre and determining the sort of experience an audience will have. Creating effective theatre is often the result of careful positioning—sometimes putting contrasting moments together and at other times putting together moments that are similar or that complement each other. Getting the structure right is a dynamic process and can keep on changing until the right order of scenes and moments is discovered.

There are different sort of structures, and you need to choose the one that best fits your piece of theatre and your intentions.

Structure can be divided into two categories.
- Narrative or story structures
- Non-narrative structures

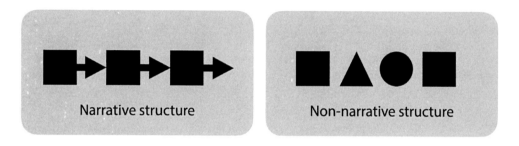

Narrative structure   Non-narrative structure

Narrative structures can vary.

- Linear narrative—one thing leads to another and the story unfolds from beginning to end
- Flashback—piece of theatre begins in the present (or at the end of the story) and then takes us back to show us how we got to this moment
- Multiple narrative—two or more stories are told at the same time
- Fragmentary—the story is told in fragments moving between different times

Non-narrative pieces of theatre do not tell a story. They usually present different ideas or perspectives. The focus of the piece of theatre could be:

- a theme
- an action
- a situation/event
- an object
- a character
- a period in history
- a setting.

The approach you choose for your own piece of theatre will be dependent on your starting point and on your theatre-maker intentions.

The following activity provides a practical way of structuring your scenes and offers a way of identifying new scenes for development.

Activity

Ordering the scenes and transitions
For this exercise you will need a piece of string that you can put up across the space to create a washing line.

- Decide whether your theatre piece should follow a narrative or non-narrative structure.
- Take the titles of each scene you created previously and write each one on an individual piece of paper.
- Put these scene titles in an order that makes sense to you and hang them on the washing line. Try using each piece of paper folded in half so that it easily hangs over the line.
- Look at this order. Discard any scenes you think may not be necessary and remove them from the washing line.
- Decide what new scenes need to be created. Write these on paper, mark them with a different colour and hang them on the line.
- Once you are happy with the structure, number the scenes on the back of the paper.
- Create any new scenes that are required.

The decisions made in the activity above will now become your planned structure for the further development of this piece of theatre. As your piece evolves and new scenes are added, the order of scenes or moments may be changed, so you can change the number on the back making sure that previous numbers remain visible.

The washing line should be photographed after each session. This will help to track the evolution of the piece of theatre, recording the changes and developments as more material is created, scenes are abandoned, and new ones are suddenly required and added. At the end of the process of creation, just by looking at the back of each piece of paper on the washing line and its position history (denoted by the changing number) you will have an at-a-glance view of how the piece has developed and been structured. This will help you with the assessment of criterion A.

Transitions
Once you have finalized the structure and content of your piece you need to turn your attention to transitions. It might be useful to also think of transitions as the glue that holds each scene together. Transitions need to be given as much attention as the scenes themselves, as these are key not only to the energy and dynamics of the piece but also to the coherence of the audience's experience.

You can think of transitions as being either:

- performer-led—the change from one scene to the next is done by the performers without relying on any production elements such as change of set, costume, lights or sound
- production element-led—the change from one scene to another is indicated by a change in a production element (costume, scenery) or a production state (lighting, sound, blackout)

You might choose one category of transition for use throughout your piece, or you might have a combination. It is a good idea to try transitioning between scenes without relying on a blackout as your piece of theatre will be so short that continuous blackouts may interrupt the pace of the piece and affect the flow.

It can be useful to think about transitions in a filmic way, and to try to theatrically replicate what we see on TV and in films, as this tends to be a more fluid and continuous experience for an audience. The following are some possible transition strategies for your scenes.

Scene transitions

Cross fade
One scene dissolves and at the same time the next scene emerges/moves into position.

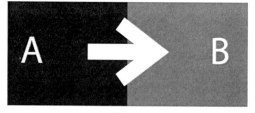

Wipe
One scene ends leaving a clear and neutral space for next scene to start.

Snap
One scene ends and another begins immediately. Very often this means that the next scene is already in position in the space.

Voiceover
One scene ends and a voiceover (often in blackout) leads the action from one scene to the next. This can be pre-recorded or live.

Motif
A transition is indicated through the use of a prop, a costume or a person—e.g we might follow a character moving from one scene into another or see a scarf that one person is wearing being transferred to another performer.

Ritual
A transition is indicated through the use of a repeated ritual—e.g. this may be text-based (i.e. particular words spoken), a chorus speech, a song/piece of music, a choreographed movement sequence.

Activity

Top and tail
Now that you have decided on your structure and the order of your scenes, you need to begin to think how all the scenes are put together to create a coherent and fluid piece.

- Run each scene and concentrate on the start of it and the end of it. Create a still image or freeze-frame of the beginning and end of each scene, with the performers momentarily holding their positions.
- Go through the sequence of the piece. Decide how the freeze-frame that is at the end of one scene transforms into the one that is the beginning of the next scene in the sequence. Consider the following questions to help formulate the best method of transitioning between each scene.

  ☑ Where do the performers need to move from and to, and how will they get there?
  ☑ What sort of style, speed or quality of movement is most appropriate to help take the performer from one point to the next? Should this be in character? Should this be visible to the audience? Should it happen extremely fast, or should it be a slow and deliberate movement?
  ☑ What other production elements might be deployed to aid with this transition? Music? Lighting? Projection? What will most help the audience understand the context of the next scene as it is establishing?
  ☑ How will key set pieces, props or materials get moved to the correct places? Who is responsible for what? How can these necessary elements be integrated into the transition as seamlessly as possible? Are they really needed?

- Rehearse moving from each scene-end to the next scene-start, deciding on the energy and the pace of each transition, as these may vary.
- When you have rehearsed these transitions and everyone is happy with them, write the details of the transitions down on coloured pieces of paper and add them to the washing line, in between each scene.

Openings and endings
Once you have your whole structure in place you can now think about the opening and ending of the piece.

The opening transports the audience into the world of the play. It is a key part of audience engagement as well as establishing how you want the audience to experience the play.

The ending is the final moment that the audience will carry with them out of the theatre and back into their lives. This will be what remains of the experience, so you need to carefully consider whether you want them to leave with a feeling, a thought, an image or a question.

30 seconds

- Look at the opening scene and final scene of the piece you have created. Decide if these are in fact the opening and the ending or if something needs to be added to the start of, or before, the first scene and to the end of, or after, the final scene (these are sometimes referred to as prologues and epilogues).
- Take two sheets of paper. Title one "opening" and the other "ending". Number each sheet of paper 1–30. Divide the paper into two columns. One column should be titled "Action" and the other "Audience".
- Examine each second of the first and last 30 seconds of the piece. Describe what happens and any production elements that are used in the column marked "Action". In the column marked "Audience" explain what you want the audience to experience in terms of the following.

  ☑ Emotion
  ☑ Thought
  ☑ Senses
  ☑ Overall experience

5.5 Staging: Performing moments of tension, emotion, atmosphere and/or meaning

The use of performance skills to create moments of tension, emotion, atmosphere and/or meaning ("TEAM") is an effective way for you to consider the application of your performance skills. This section addresses the significance and power of the performer and their ability to transport the audience to different places, show them different emotional states or have them sitting on the edge of their seats simply through the use of body and voice.

For the collaborative project task, every student is assessed.

- The extent to which **you use your performance skills** to effectively contribute to one moment of "TEAM" as visible in two minutes of the video recording of the piece of theatre. The two minutes is chosen by you.
- The extent to which you **explain how you use your performance** skills to effectively contribute to one moment of "TEAM" as visible in two minutes of the video recording.

Therefore, it is important to make sure that there is one moment of at least two minutes in the final piece of theatre the ensemble has created that showcases your performance skills and the way you have used them to create a moment of "TEAM".

Throughout the theatre course you should be developing your performance skills and finding opportunities to perform in a variety of roles and performances. The best way to acquire and develop skills is through practice.

"TEAM"

- Take a look at the scenes you have already created as an ensemble in the previous exercises and identify the ones you performed in or any that you are planning to perform in.
- Choose one of the scenes that you perform in that you think would be suitable for assessment. It should be two minutes long and include a moment of "TEAM". If you cannot identify one scene, then you will need to discuss this with your ensemble and create more material.
- Choose which of the four aspects of "TEAM" this moment is most concerned with. Once you have identified one aspect (e.g. a moment of meaning showing friendship), write a list of as many ways as you can think of that the body and voice can be used to create this aspect of the moment, using the space below.

- Create a collage of images that you have sourced (photographs, art, portraits) that show this particular aspect (e.g. images of friendship).
- Find audio that you think might contribute aurally to this moment (e.g. friends in conversation, laughter).
- Write a list of words related to this aspect (e.g. companionship, kindness, consideration, humour).
- You will now have a "thesaurus" of the moment, made up of words, images and sounds. This is almost like a list of ingredients.
- Use this to inform your performance and re-do the scene with these elements in mind.
- Ask someone outside the group to be your audience member. Explain what sort of moment you are trying to create.

- Perform the moment.
- Ask your audience to feed back on how effectively they think you have performed the aspect of the moment you set out to communicate.
- Use all the information you have from this exercise to explain how you have used performance elements to create this moment of "TEAM" (using the space below).

Activity

Enhancing your performance
- Write a list of all the elements of performance that this moment involves (e.g. voice, volume, gesture, facial expression).
- Research performance skills and find one exercise to suit you that develops each of the areas you have identified.
- If you are playing a character, consider the character's identity, background, physicality, posture, movement, way of talking, emotional state, etc.
- Research activities for, and approaches to, developing a character and use these to develop your character.
- Ask a partner to take a photograph of you at five different moments in the scene.
- Examine each of these and write a list of what you need to further enhance or highlight regarding your posture and body.
- Record any text you are speaking.
- Listen to the recording and write a list of what you need to further enhance or highlight regarding your vocal skills.
- Ask someone to film the scene containing your two minutes.
- Watch this and identify what you need to do to enhance your performance.
- Take time to focus on each of the areas you have identified. Remember your performance will be watched by the examiner on film so make sure that your performance includes everything you want them to see.

- Perform the piece to someone and ask them to give you feedback regarding your:

  - ☑ use of voice
  - ☑ articulation
  - ☑ volume
  - ☑ pace
  - ☑ use of body
  - ☑ use of face
  - ☑ use of gesture
  - ☑ posture
  - ☑ movement
  - ☑ energy/feeling
  - ☑ characterization (if appropriate).

- Use all the information you have from this exercise to evaluate how effectively you have used performance elements to create this moment of "TEAM", using the space below.

5.6 Staging: Directing, designing and production elements

Contribution to the staging of a piece of theatre as a director or designer requires you to think about how you will work with performers and/or production elements to fulfil the ensemble's theatre-maker intentions. The experience that the audience will have and the effect you want the piece to have on the audience is key. In this respect, in these roles you will be constantly viewing the material through the eyes of the audience and making decisions using this perspective. You will also be constantly referring to the collaborative theatre-maker intentions.

Introducing production elements often lifts and improves the staging of the piece of theatre. Very simple production elements used well and with intention can often be more effective than complicated lighting rigs, costume and set changes. The brief in the *Theatre guide* for this task is for a low-budget, touring production, so keep this in mind as you work. This will help you avoid getting distracted by spending unnecessary amounts of time on the construction of scenery or the making of costumes. This is where returning to your theatre-maker intentions is helpful to make sure you do not get absorbed in production elements that are not essential.

The following activities are designed to engage you in the process of staging through the eyes of director and designer.

Activity

Directing

In this activity you will working on one of the scenes that were previously created by the ensemble or by you and your partner. If the scene you will be working on as a director is also one that you are performing in (which can happen if the ensemble is small) then you might want to film the scene. This will give you the opportunity to watch it and make decisions based on the recording or you could ask someone to stand in for you so that you get to see the scene live.

- Think about the role of the director and write a short list of what you think are the:
  - ☑ key responsibilities for a director of a collaboratively created piece of original theatre
  - ☑ actions a director takes.

- Choose one of the scenes created in the earlier exercises.
- Read the collaboratively written theatre-maker intentions to remind yourself of what you are trying to achieve as a director.
- Using the space provided overleaf, identify how you think this scene contributes to the realization of the ensemble's theatre-making intentions. Which aspects of the intentions does it most contribute to?
- Write a director intention that focuses only on the scene you are working on. Sometimes, for example, the scene you will be directing might be highlighting the ensemble's intentions through contrast (e.g. a surreal scene in an otherwise naturalistic piece of theatre).

The responsibilities of the director

Director's intention for the scene

- Look at the list you wrote regarding the responsibilities and actions of a director and create a directing plan regarding the performers, the space and any production elements.
- Begin with the opening moment of the scene and the final moment of scene. Look at each of these and direct the scene as if it is a journey that takes us from the opening moment to the final moment.
- You might also want to try the following strategies to give you new perspectives or ideas.

  - ☑ Change the pace
  - ☑ Change the style
  - ☑ Change the space
  - ☑ Add a new gesture
  - ☑ Add a new line of text
  - ☑ Add an object or piece of set

- When you have finished working on the direction of the scene, complete the chart below/opposite. Use this as a guide to explain how you directed this scene in order to effectively fulfil the ensemble's theatre-maker intentions and the desired effect on the audience.

How this scene contributes to the ensemble's collaborative theatre-maker intentions

My theatre-maker intentions for this scene

What I did to achieve this

Action 1

Action 2

Action 3

Action 4

**How I directed this scene to effectively fulfil the
ensemble's theatre-maker intentions and the desired effect on the audience.**

Design and use of production elements

Remember that your piece of originally created theatre is a low-budget, touring production. For this activity, imagine it will be going on a tour to:

- ☑ another school (that does not have a dedicated performance space)
- ☑ a small theatre space without fixed seating
- ☑ a community space without performance facilities but set in a large open area.

- Begin by reflecting on the role of the designer and the difference between technical design (e.g. sound, lights) and scenic design (e.g. set, costume).
- Choose which areas of design you want to focus on for this task (e.g. set, costume, lights, sound, special effects).
- Read the collaboratively written theatre-maker intentions to remind yourself of what you are trying to achieve as a designer.
- Begin by drawing the shape of your performance space and the positioning of your audience in the box opposite, labelled 'My performance space'. Think about how this space will be marked out in the spaces you are touring to (e.g. lights, floor cloth, chairs).
- Indicate on your drawing any pieces of set that you have already decided as an ensemble are in the space.
- Choose one of the scenes created in the earlier exercises. Draw a visual plan of what the performance space looks like for the scene you are directing, in the second box labelled 'My performance space for my chosen scene'. What changes are there in this scene which are different from the overall plan and set design?
- Identify how you think this scene contributes to the realization of the ensemble's theatre-making intentions. Which aspects of the intentions does it most contribute to?
- Write a designer intention that focuses only on the scene you are working on and on your production element(s) of choice. Sometimes, for example, the scene you will be designing is trying to set a particular type of atmosphere.
- You can now begin to practically work on design through any or a combination of the following.

  - ☑ Set—create an actual set for the scene using tables, chairs and found objects in the space. Photograph this.
  - ☑ Lights—light the entire scene using only torches, electronic devices, household lamps and candles.
  - ☑ Costume—source images that give a sense of colour, texture, shape, style of costume(s) and create a collage showing this. Remember to keep it simple as you will have to make or source the costumes.
  - ☑ Sound—create the soundtrack for the scene by selecting appropriate music and/or sound effects or composing your own.

- Arrange for the scene to be performed and record it. Add a voiceover to the recording explaining how, as a designer, you used production elements to effectively contribute to the fulfilment of the ensemble's intentions.
- Discuss with your partner or ensemble how a designer contributes to the staging of a piece of theatre and what this contribution involves. How are intentions met through design?

My performance space

My performance space for my chosen scene

Designer's intention

5.7 Audience feedback and evaluation

Feedback from an audience is a key requirement of the collaborative project assessment task.

For the collaborative project, feedback is not being given in order to help you to improve the piece. Rather, the feedback is required to help you gather evidence to support your evaluation of the extent to which the piece of theatre met its original intentions. It is important, therefore, to decide in advance how to gather and record feedback that will be most useful for your evaluation and that will help you to meet the criteria of the assessment task. Generating questions that will provoke the feedback you want and finding the best ways to elicit and capture this is an improtant part of this syllabus area.

You can think of questions as "open" or "closed". Closed questions are often yes or no questions or questions that will only give you brief answers. Open questions will give you more information. Open questions, for example, can begin with the following.

- How do you think …?
- To what extent did ….?
- What did you think was …?
- What was effective about …?

Audience feedback
- Look at the elements of your collaboratively created theatre-maker intentions.
- Develop a series of questions related to each aspect of your intentions using the spaces below/overleaf.

Area of collaborative theatre-maker intentions	Question
Purpose	
Message/theme/ideas	
Effect on audience	
Performance space	
Use of performance elements	
Use of production elements	
Moments of "TEAM"	
Key moments	
Other	

- You may also want to get specific information about your individual performance or your contribution to directing or designing. Create questions for these using the space provided below/overleaf.

Area of individual performance	Question
Use of body	
Use of voice	

Use of performance space	
Effect on audience	
Creation of moments of "TEAM"	
Most effective aspects	
Other	

Area of contribution to directing/designing	Question
Use of performers	
How performance and production elements worked together	
Use of performance space	
Effect on audience	
Creation of moments of "TEAM"	
Most effective aspects	
Other	

- Think about different ways you can share your theatre-maker intentions with an audience (e.g. programme notes) and also how you will organize the way you get feedback.
- Examine the following approaches to getting audience feedback and write notes on how you will capture feedback so that you can refer to it during the process of evaluating your work.

Approaches to capturing feedback

Approach	Possible ways to gather and record feedback with this approach
Talk-back with the ensemble as a panel taking comments from the audience as a whole	
Individual members of the ensemble interview individual members of the audience	
Audience divided into small groups and small-group discussions led by each individual member of the ensemble	
Survey handed out after the production	
Survey sent to audience at another time	
Audience members write their responses to the production and place them in a designated area after the performance	
Digital forum/feedback space that the audience is given access to	
Other	

Definition: Talk-back
A talk-back happens after the performance is over. The audience stay behind and have the chance to ask questions or discuss the play with the performers, creators, directors and/or designers.

Evaluation

Self-reflection and evaluation is an important skill for all theatre-makers as it is the process that helps you to develop as an artist. The assessment task requires you to evaluate two areas of your contribution to the piece of theatre, focusing on two different moments that you will select from the final piece. Each moment cannot be longer than two minutes.

Activity

Reflection and evaluation

This activity is focussed on the piece of theatre you have created in the previous activities.

- Reflect on your contributions how, as a:

  ☑ performer, you feel you effectively contributed to one moment of "TEAM"

  ☑ creator, you feel you successfully contributed to the creation/ development of the moment of action to fulfil the ensemble's intentions

  ☑ director and/or designer, you feel you successfully contributed to the staging of the moment of action to fulfil the ensemble's intentions.

- Complete the two tables opposite, providing evidence of your contribution to each area listed. What did you feel was effective? What did you find challenging?
- Share these notes with a partner explaining your evaluation of yourself as a performer and your evaluation of your contributions to the development and to the staging of particular moments of action.
- Using the spaces below, identify how you contributed to the final performance piece and what some of the challenges were that you faced along the way.

Evaluation of my contributions

As creator

As performer

As director

As designer

Identifying contributions to the final performance piece	
The spirit and success of the ensemble	
The overall creation of the piece	
The overall staging of the piece as a performer	
The overall staging of the piece as a designer or director	

Identifying challenges faced	
Working as part of an ensemble	
In the creation of the piece	
As a performer	
As a designer and/or director	

- Regarding the final piece of theatre, use these reflections to write an overall evaluation of your contribution to its:

    1. creation
    2. development
    3. staging.

5.8 Preparing for assessment: Recording the performance, writing the report and completing the cover sheet

For the assessment of this task you need to have:

- a completed cover sheet
- a project report (a maximum of 10 pages of written text and images) plus a list of all sources used
- a video recording of the final piece (7–10 minutes maximum).

The video recording

Having created and staged the piece you need to arrange how it will be recorded as you are required to submit a full recording of the piece for assessment. Deciding how the piece will be recorded will be discussed with your teacher.

The *Theatre guide* provides information regarding the nature of the final recording of the piece.

What the guide says

Video recording
The full performance of the theatre piece must be captured in a video recording that is submitted for assessment (lasting 7–10 minutes) by each member of the ensemble. This must be a continuous, single-camera, unedited record and must capture the full presentation of the piece from the best vantage point possible. The video recording device must not be switched off during the performance.

As the one single video recording is used to assess the effectiveness of the performance skills and artistic contributions of each member of the ensemble it is crucial that all action can be clearly seen and heard in the recording. The video camera should avoid unnecessary panning or zooming during the performance.

In preparing to video record the assessed piece teachers are encouraged to allow students time to walk through their performance prior to filming to give the operator of the video recording device an indication of how the space will be used and the most appropriate way of positioning the camera to frame the whole performance from a fixed position.

As you can see, there are some important things for you to bear in mind.

- The camera is fixed.
- There is one single recording without any stops.
- Unnecessary panning or zooming should be avoided.
- The film cannot be edited.

From this video recording you will need to choose two different moments of two minutes each, as follows.

Moment 1: Performance

This will show the examiner to what extent your performance skills (body and/or voice) effectively contribute to a moment of "TEAM" seen in the video recording (as specified by the student in section 2(a) of the project report).

Moment 2: Artistic development or staging

This will show the examiner to what extent your own individual contributions to the artistic development and/or staging of the piece as creator, designer and/or director (as specified by the student in section 2(b) of the project report) effectively contribute to the fulfilment of the ensemble's intentions within the context of the whole video recording.

Choosing your two moments is key. This is specified and highlighted in the *Theatre guide*.

What the guide says

Selecting moments for assessment

Students must ensure that the two moments they select will provide sufficient evidence of their performance skills and their individual artistic contributions respectively, as well as meeting the requirements of the task and providing sufficient opportunities for them to address the assessment criteria.

This means that you must ensure that your contributions are clearly visible and audible in the recording.

To ensure you give yourself the best chance for success in this task, consider the following advice.

- Choose your moments carefully.
- Make sure when the piece is being created that there is enough individual material for you to be assessed.
- Bear in mind when you are creating the piece that it will be recorded and adjust your performance and artistic contributions to take this into consideration.
- Think about the visibility and volume (if you are using voice) of your performance.
- Arrange for a recording to be made of a rehearsal with the camera in the same position that it will be in for the final recording so you can watch it and make any adjustments that are needed.

The cover sheet

The cover sheet is an essential part of the assessment as it provides the examiner with key information regarding:

- how they can identify you
- the ensemble's collaboratively created intentions that will be the standard against which your work will be judged
- the time stamps that tells the examiner which two moments you wish them to focus on. In other words, you are choosing what you want to be assessed on for criteria B and C.

What the guide says

Cover sheet

A cover sheet is provided by the IB for this task and a completed cover sheet must be submitted for each student as part of the upload of assessment materials. Failure to submit the cover sheet will result in the work not being marked.

The cover sheet records the following information for this task.

- ☑ How the student can be identified in the video recording (including a screenshot of the student).
- ☑ The ensemble's chosen starting point for the piece.
- ☑ The collaboratively written theatre-maker intentions.
- ☑ The page count of the submitted report. All text images, annotations, labels and citations must be included in the overall page count.
- ☑ The length of the submitted video recording.
- ☑ The specific beginning and ending time codes that direct the examiner to the student's two chosen moments in the submitted video recording.

The project report

The project report (10 pages of written text and images, with written text not exceeding 4,000 words maximum) is a written account of your involvement in the collaborative project. The project report does not follow the chronological process followed by the ensemble during the collaborative creation of the final pieces. As such, the structure of the report should not dictate the process you follow.

There are two sections to the report. Each section has a recommended maximum length of 5 pages and can include visuals.

What the guide says

Structuring the report

Section one: The collaborative creative process and performance

a. Each student provides their own individual explanation of how the piece was collaboratively created by the ensemble, referencing significant instances from the process. Please note: reflecting on the collaborative creative process does not mean that students should see this as an opportunity to complain, blame or criticize other members of the ensemble.

b. After the piece is performed, and with reference to audience feedback, each student evaluates the effectiveness of the final piece as a whole, explaining how they consider the ensemble's intentions were achieved.

Section two: Individual contributions to the performance

a. After watching the video recording of the final piece, each student explains how they used their performance skills (body and/or voice) to effectively contribute to one specific and effective moment of tension, emotion, atmosphere and/or meaning ("TEAM") visible in the video recording. The chosen moment must not exceed two minutes maximum and the time codes for this moment must be stated on the cover sheet. Each student must clearly state which element(s) of "TEAM" they will be addressing in the chosen moment.

b. After watching the video recording of the final piece, each student explains how their own specific individual artistic contributions to the development and/or staging of the piece as creator, designer and/or director (outside of their performance moment described above) effectively contributed to the fulfilment of the ensemble's intentions in one moment seen in the video recording. This moment must be a different moment in the piece to the one described above and must not exceed two minutes maximum. The time codes must be stated on the cover sheet. Each student must clearly state which role(s) they made their artistic contributions in (creator, designer and/or director) for the one moment.

Top tip
Section two of the project report requires you to watch the video recording and use this as the basis of your reflections and evaluation

---

Collaborative project assessment criteria

Criterion A: The collaborative creative process and performance
Evidence: cover sheet, project report and list of sources

  i.   With reference to significant instances from the process, to what extent does the student explain how they consider the piece was collaboratively created by the ensemble?
  ii. With reference to audience feedback, to what extent does the student evaluate the effectiveness of the final piece as a whole, in relation to how they consider the ensemble's intentions were achieved?

What the examiner wants to see
Criterion A(i)
● That you understand how an original piece of theatre is collaboratively created
● That you can reflect on and explain the process that you and your ensemble adopted
● That you can identify moments of success and moments of challenge and explain what made these significant in the process

Criterion A(ii)
● That you evaluate the extent to which you think the piece met its original intentions referring to the elements of this intention (e.g. target audience, themes/ideas, performance space, effect on audience)
● That you have evidence of audience feedback and that you have used this to inform your evaluation
● That you can evaluate how effective what the ensemble created and staged was as a piece of theatre

---

Collaborative project assessment criteria

Criterion B: Individual contributions to the performance
Evidence: cover sheet, project report and list of sources

  i.   To what extent does the student explain how they used their performance skills (body and/or voice) to effectively contribute to one moment of tension, emotion, atmosphere and/or meaning ("TEAM") visible in the video recording? (This moment must not exceed two minutes maximum and the time codes must be stated on the cover sheet.)
  ii. To what extent does the student explain how their specific individual artistic contribution(s) to the development and staging of the piece as creator, designer and/or director effectively contributed to the fulfilment of the ensemble's intentions in one moment seen in the video recording? (This moment must be a **different** moment in the piece from the one described above and must not exceed two minutes maximum. The time codes must be stated on the cover sheet.)

What the examiner wants to see
Criterion B(i)

- That you understand how performance skills can be used to effectively create a moment of "TEAM"
- That you can explain your choices regarding the use of performance skills
- That you know how to use performance skills effectively to create a moment of "TEAM"

Criterion B(ii)

- That you have contributed to the development and/or staging of the piece as a creator, designer and/or director
- That you understand the process of your chosen role (as creator, designer and/or director)
- That you can explain your contribution and why you think this has added to the effectiveness of the whole piece and to the fulfilment of the ensemble's intentions

---

Collaborative project assessment criteria

Criterion C: Effectiveness of individual contributions seen in the video recording

Evidence: cover sheet and video recording

   i.   To what extent do the student's performance skills (body and/or voice) effectively contribute to a moment of tension, emotion, atmosphere and/or meaning ("TEAM") seen in the video recording (as specified by the student in section 2(a) of the project report)?

   ii.   To what extent do the student's own individual contributions to the artistic development and/or staging of the piece as creator, designer and/or director (as specified by the student in section 2(b) of the project report) effectively contribute to the fulfilment of the ensemble's intentions within the context of the whole recording?

What the examiner wants to see
Criterion C(i)

- That you can effectively use your performance skills (body and/or voice) in a live performance
- That you are able to effectively contribute to the moment of "TEAM" that you described in your project report

Criterion C(ii)

- That your contributions to the development and/or staging of the piece as a creator, designer and/or director are visible in the video recording of the live performance
- That your contributions effectively add to the whole piece and to the fulfilment of the ensemble's intentions

Chapter 5: Recap

In this chapter we have explored the topic of collaboratively creating original theatre, focusing on:

- building an ensemble and advice on choosing a starting point for an original piece of theatre

- approaches for exploring a starting point and recommendations for generating theatre-maker intentions

- the role of the creator and strategies for generating original performance material

- practical strategies for performing effective moments of "TEAM"

- staging an original piece of theatre through direction, design and production elements

- the importance of audience feedback and possible approaches for recording responses from audience members

- the requirements of the collaborative project assessment task and how to prepare materials for submission to the IB.

6. Performing theatre theory and the solo theatre piece (HL only)

> While the performing theatre theory syllabus area and solo theatre piece assessment task are intended for higher level (HL) students only, this section is also useful for standard level (SL) students wishing to further develop their theatre skills.

You can either work individually, in pairs or in small groups for all of the activities in this chapter.

Introduction

This chapter addresses the following areas of performing theatre theory.

6.1   Choosing and researching a theatre theorist and their overarching intentions
6.2   Researching and exploring an aspect of theatre theory
6.3   Developing theatre-maker intentions
6.4   Performance material and the process of developing the piece
6.5   Feedback and evaluation
6.6   Preparing for assessment: Structuring your report and recording your performance

The performing theatre theory syllabus area is designed to introduce you to the high-level skill of engaging with theatre theory and using this to inform your practice. Theatre theory is made up of frameworks, approaches, techniques and models of practice that have been developed by a theatre theorist. It is the study of theatrical discoveries, changes and innovations that have contributed to the development of contemporary theatre and to theatre over time. Theory informs how theatre is made, its purpose and the effect it has on an audience.

This area of the syllabus aims to develop your understanding of the value of theatre theory and the insights it provides into theatre as a form of art. It is important to understand that theatre theory is related to practice, to the process of making and presenting theatre, as well as to the analysis of theatre from an audience's perspective. This syllabus area and the solo theatre piece assessment task also brings together all the different theatre-making skills and understandings of the course, requiring you to engage with theatre as a performer, a creator, a designer and a director. It also gives you the opportunity to make the theatre you want to make, based on a theatre theorist whose ideas and theories resonate with your own.

Theatre theory also gives you the opportunity to access what may sometimes seem like abstract or impenetrable theatre. It can provide you with a key to unlock new ideas, to understand the purpose of theatrical experiments and to engage with aspects of theatre you might never have encountered. Anyone wishing to study theatre beyond high school is often required to engage with theatre theory.

> **Definition: Theatre theory**
> Theatre theory is theory that is directly related to the creation, purpose, performance and presentation of theatre. It encompasses ideas about theatre as an art form, genre and style. It can also refer to theatre processes and theatre practices.

> **Definition: Aspect of theory**
> An aspect of theatre theory refers to one particular area of a theatre theorist's work. It may be an idea, a process, a stylistic element, a convention, a technique or an approach.

Aspect of theory

The focus of the culminating assessment task—the solo theatre piece—is an aspect of a theorist's theory.

It is important to note that this syllabus area is designed to give you an understanding of an aspect(s) of theatre theory and its relationship to practice. You are not required to create a piece of theatre that shows every single aspect of a theorist's theory.

The aspect(s) of theatre theory you choose should be something that typifies a particular theatre theorist's work and should be narrow enough to provide you with the opportunity to really delve deeply into it. In this respect, this syllabus area is about depth and not breadth. It encourages a focused, microscopic engagement with an aspect of theory, rather than a broad, generalist overview.

Furthermore, whatever aspect(s) you choose needs to be noticeably demonstrated in the piece of theatre you create and perform.

> **Definition: Solo theatre piece**
> A piece of theatre created, designed, directed and performed by an individual.

Making solo performance work

The solo theatre piece is designed to develop your performance and production skills, so it is important to consider this area as being not only about exploring, understanding and working with theatre theory but also about developing your performance and production skills.

You will need to feel confident and comfortable with the idea of performing on your own, so this needs to be a key part of your work in this syllabus area. Whether working with existing written monologues or devising short one-person scenes, give yourself lots of opportunities to perform solo to your peers or to an external audience. This will help build your confidence.

> **Top tip**
> Sharing your work with others is a significant way to gain feedback to help you develop your solo theatre piece. It is important for you to organize to share work-in-progress and to ask for feedback and audience responses.

In the final assessment task, **you must** also design all elements of production; however, you are permitted to have others construct or arrange production elements following your designs and specifications. Although this is a solo performance, you are still required to collaborate in order to benefit your work.

This syllabus area is an exciting opportunity for you to explore theatre theory, have complete artistic freedom and create a piece of theatre that you want to create.

What the guide says

For the solo theatre piece assessment task each student is required to submit the following.

- A report (2,500 words maximum) plus a list of all primary and secondary sources cited.
- A continuous unedited video recording of the whole solo theatre piece (lasting 4–7 minutes maximum).

To achieve this, the solo theatre piece task requires you to undertake the following process.

- Carry out research on a theatre theorist you have not previously studied, explore a specific theory presented by that theorist, with a focus on the theorist's overarching intentions and the nature of their theatre practice (which may be theatrical, social, political, philosophical and so on).
- Formulate theatre-maker intentions for the creation of a solo theatre piece that demonstrates the practical application of your chosen aspect(s) of theatre theory. Your theatre-maker intentions should be aligned with the theatre theorist's overarching intentions.
- Undertake a process of developing your solo theatre piece, led by your theatre–maker intentions. You will practically apply the selected aspect(s) of your chosen theory and incorporate performance and/or production elements to create, design and rehearse your solo theatre piece in order to fulfil your stated intentions.
- Perform the final solo theatre piece (lasting 4–7 minutes) to a live audience.
- Gather feedback from the audience to assess the extent to which the piece fulfilled your theatre-maker intentions.
- Evaluate the effectiveness of the presented solo theatre piece in terms of your theatre-maker intentions and the extent to which these have been met or have not.
- Write your report.

Assessment criteria
The solo theatre piece is assessed using the following criteria.

	Solo theatre piece	Marks	Total
A	Researching theatre theory	8	
B	Reflecting on the performed solo theatre piece	8	24
C	Theatre theory in performance	8	

The activities outlined in this chapter have been designed to fully prepare you for success in each of these areas.

6.1 Choosing and researching a theatre theorist and their overarching intentions

Theatre theorists present their ideas for a purpose and because they believe in and are passionate about developing or changing a particular type of theatre.

Overarching intentions

The *Theatre guide* explains that the theatre theorist's overarching intentions may be theatrical, social, political, philosophical and so on. In other words, their intentions may go beyond theatre.

Definition: Theatre theorist
A theatre practitioner who has contributed to the shaping and development of theatre through their published work and ideas (primary sources). In addition, there are published works by others (secondary sources) regarding the theatre theorist's contributions, ideas and the effect they have had on theatre practice. This signifies that the theatre theorist's work has had implications beyond their own practice and on theatre in general.

Discovering a theatre theorist's overarching intentions (the sort of effect they want their theatre to have on the world) is a key part of this task. This is key because it will:

a. help you to choose which theatre theorist you want to explore
b. inform the making of your piece of theatre, as your intentions need to be in line with the theatre theorist's intentions.

Finding the right theorist will also ignite your interest and allow you to create the sort of theatre you want to make. Identifying your passion in theatre is a great place to start before choosing a theatre theorist.

You might want to choose a theatre theorist who resonates with you and who will provide you with ideas and principles to make the sort of theatre you want to make, or you may want to explore a theatre theory whose ideas you find interesting.

Whatever you decide, the final assessment task—the solo theatre piece—should feel like a passion project; after all, this is an independent project that gives you ultimate artistic responsibility and freedom.

Activity

Your theatre-making mission
This activity helps you to think about the role that theatre can play in different societies, communities and cultures, and the sort of theatre you want to make.

- Consider each of the following and decide which ones interest you the most. Think about the reasons why these might be the most appealing for you personally.

  - ☑ Entertainment
  - ☑ Musical theatre
  - ☑ Political theatre
  - ☑ Community theatre
  - ☑ Revivals
  - ☑ Experimental theatre
  - ☑ New writing
  - ☑ Immersive theatre
  - ☑ Provocative theatre
  - ☑ Productions of classics
  - ☑ Verbatim
  - ☑ Live art

- Using the spaces provided opposite, consider what you believe the role of theatre should be and the sort of theatre you want to make (your 'theatre mission').
- With a partner, present your 'theatre mission' and argue for the sort of theatre you want to make, justifying your reasons and arguing that this is the most important form of theatre. These would be your overarching intentions regarding your own theatre-making.

Theatre mission: The theatre I think should be made	
I believe theatre should …	
The main aspect of this sort of theatre would be …	
This sort of theatre would take place in …	
Performers would … in order to …	
The main production elements would be … in order to …	
As a result of this sort of theatre audiences would …	
I would call this theatre …	

Now that you have thought about the sort of theatre you want to make, we will examine how theatre theory is transformed into action.

A theatre theorist's overarching intentions

This activity provides you with theoretical statements that describe a theorist's overarching intentions. Alongside each statement is an appropriate starting point to help guide you as you begin making theatre based on theory.

- Look at the list of theoretical statements and starting points below.
- Choose one of the statements/intentions from this list. Use the provided starting point to create a two-minute solo scene that clearly demonstrates the theoretical statement and the theorist's overarching intention.
- Present your scene to a partner and ask them to guess what the theory might be.
- Discuss the following.

  ☑ How visible was the theory in the piece of theatre?
  ☑ How can theory be used to create theatre?
  ☑ How did you approach making theatre based on theory?
  ☑ What was most challenging?

Theoretical overarching intentions

1) "When theatre is at its best it undermines everything we know and opens up the world so that we see what we have never seen before. It uses nothing but the human form moving in space because words hide more than they reveal."

Starting point: Poverty

2) "What is the body but a giant megaphone through which words are spoken, images drawn and songs are sung? Give me stillness, give me text, make me a listener. I am too, too tired of this busy world of looking and seeing and watching."

Starting point: Empty chairs

3) "Let there be joy and celebration, a pageant and a parade, singing and dancing, things to make my spirit rise and fly not plummet and sink. Theatre has become far too serious. Make me tap my toes and click my fingers, let performers be performers and let them lead us in the dance."

Starting point: A myth or fairytale

4) "The edge between the light and dark, where the spotlight ends and the darkness begins. That fine line. This is all the action that we need, this play of light and shadow, colour and shape that stays on the retina long after the show is over. This is our life, this should be our theatre, our emergence into light and our dive into the dark."

Starting point: Mazu, the sea goddess

5) "Wake up! This is not theatre, this is real life. Take up arms! Change the world. Look at what we have done. Forget the silly stories and the fancy sets. Make it real. Make it matter. Do not sit me down in comfy seats, wake me up and get me up. Make it real. Make it matter."

Starting point: An artwork by street artist Banksy

Theatre theorists

The *Theatre guide* defines a theatre theorist as a theatre practitioner who has contributed to the shaping and development of theatre. In other words, someone who has changed the theatre practice or tradition of their time.

The development of theatre theory is the result of a vision by a theatre practitioner of how theatre practice can be enhanced, changed or developed. In this respect, it is essential that you understand the cultural, social, political and/or historical context of the theorist and the theatre that was common or that was emerging during the time when they were practising. This will help you to understand their legacy and their position in current theatre practice.

It is a good idea for you to have some broad sense of the many different theatre theorists that there are, their contributions to theatre practice and their overarching intentions. This will help you to make your choice of theatre theorist for the final assessment task.

Below are some theatre theorists that appear as examples in the *Theatre guide*.

Possible primary source
- Book: *The Viewpoints Book* by Bogart and Landau (2004)

Possible secondary source
- Book: *Anne Bogart: View Points* by Dixon and Smith (1995)

Anne Bogart (b.1951)

Possible primary source
- Interview: "Connecting Flights: Robert Lepage in Conversation with Rémy Charest" (1998)

Possible secondary source
- Book: *The Theatricality of Robert Lepage* by Dundjerović (2007)

Robert Lepage (b.1957)

Possible primary source
- Book: *On the Art of No Drama: The Major Treatises of Zeami* translated by Yamazaki and Rimer (1984)

Possible secondary source
- Book: *Zeami: Performance Notes* by Zeami and Hare (2011)

Zeami Motokiyo (b.1363)

Julie Taymor (b.1952)

> **Possible primary source**
> - Book: *Julie Taymor: Playing with Fire* by Blumenthal, Taymor and Monda (2007)
>
> **Possible secondary source**
> - Book: *The Re-emergence of Mythology, Fantasy and Fable* by Stewart (2009)

Robert Wilson (b.1941)

> **Possible primary source**
> - Lecture: "1. Have you been here before? 2. No this is the first time" (2008)
>
> **Possible secondary source**
> - Book: *Robert Wilson: From Within* by Safir (2011)

Definition: Sources
These are published or recorded material of the theorist's actual words (primary sources) communicating their theatre theory, along with published or recorded materials by others (secondary sources) writing or speaking about the theorist's work.

Activity

Choosing a theatre theorist
- Look through the list of theatre theorists presented above. Choose one of these theorists (or choose one from your own research) and try to locate the suggested sources. You may also consult alternative sources if you find them. Your chosen theorist will be used for the following set of activities, so be sure you feel comfortable with your choice.
- Consult primary and secondary sources on your chosen theorist and try to gain an understanding of the cultural, social, political and/or historical context the theorist was working in when they were making theatre. Make notes in your theatre journal.

Activity

Theatre theorist taster
- Using your chosen theatre theorist and your research into their context, plan a 5–10-minute presentation that introduces the theorist to others.
- Research and define the theatre theorist's overarching intentions regarding what they believe theatre should do and how they want an audience to experience it. Use the "Researching your theorist" diagram opposite to guide the development of your presentation, and record your findings in the spaces provided overleaf.
- Your presentation should include the following.

1. An introduction to the theatre theorist and their context
2. An introduction to the theatre theorist's overarching intentions
3. An overview of their key theories using, where possible, the theorist's own words (primary sources)
4. Their impact on theatre practice (secondary sources)
5. An outline of the theatre theorist's performance style and an explanation of the aesthetics of the theatre theorist's form of theatre (what a performance looks and sounds like)

- The presentation can be in any format—for example, slide show (images and text), practical demonstration, live action. It must be accompanied by a handout with five key pieces of information in the form of written notes. You must use at least one image showing what the theory might look like in action. Be sure to include a list of sources.
- Deliver your 5–10 minute introductory presentation to a partner or the rest of the class.

Researching your theorist

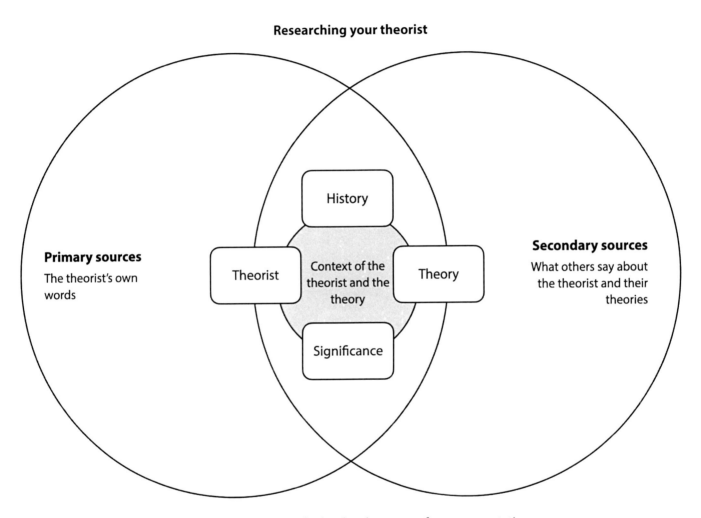

Use this diagram to guide the development of your presentation.

Findings from primary sources

What does the theorist say about their theory?

Findings from secondary sources

What do others say about the theorist and their theories?

History

What is the relationship of the theory to other theatre theories of the time that may have informed, influenced or inspired it?

Significance

What is the significance of the theory to the development of theatre subsequently?

Theatre-maker intentions

What does the theorist want their theatre to achieve?

The aesthetics of the theorist's theatre

How are elements of theatre employed to achieve the theorist's intentions?
What is the performance style? What does a performance look and sound like?

6.2 Researching and exploring an aspect of theatre theory

The solo theatre piece assessment task, as explained above, requires you to focus primarily on one, possibly two, aspects of theory. Remember, the more focused your work is, the better.

The following activities help you to identify aspect(s) of theory and take you through a process of scrutinizing, playing and experimenting with it. You will also need to consider the performance and production potential

Some example aspect(s) for each of the identified theorists are presented below and overleaf.

Anne Bogart

Example aspect(s) of theory:
Space and time

Robert Lepage

Example aspect(s) of theory:
Film projection

Zeami Motokiyo

Example aspect(s) of theory:
Quality of movement

Julie Taymor

Example aspect(s) of theory:
Use of puppets as a
device for storytelling

Robert Wilson

Example aspect(s) of theory:
Use of light

Activity

Researching aspects of theory

For the next set of activities, you will be working with either a theatre theorist of your choice, or one of the five presented earlier.

- Choose your theatre theorist and carry out research in order to identify a range of different aspects of their theory using primary and secondary sources.
- Write a list of the aspects of their theory and your sources in the two tables provided below/opposite.

Primary sources

Aspect of theory	Source	Type of source/ date accessed	Publication details	Quote/reference

Secondary sources

Aspect of theory	Source	Type of source/ date accessed	Publication details	Quote/reference

Once you have identified the aspect(s) of theory in the work of your chosen theorist, the next activity aims to bring the aspect(s) of theory alive, showing its practical and theatrical potential. It also encourages you to start thinking about aspects of theatre theory in terms of performance and production elements—in other words, the theatrical application of the aspect(s) of theory. This is ultimately what you will be assessed on.

Performance and production elements related to aspect(s) of theory
This activity will help you to consider how aspects of theory "appear" in action, on stage.

- Continuing to work with the theorist you chose in the previous activity, choose one aspect(s) of theory to focus on.
- Find out what the aspect(s) of theory you identified might look like in performance. You can research this by looking at images, photographs, written accounts, interviews or filmed performances. This will give you a sense of how this aspect(s) has previously been interpreted and applied to stage action.
- Identify as many performance and production elements as you can relating to one of the aspects of theory. Using the prompts and spaces presented on the next four pages, complete as many as you can for your chosen aspect. Feel free to use sketched drawings and diagrams in addition to words.

Activity

Performance and production elements

1. What performance space would be used?
Source

2. Where would a performer be placed in the performance space?
Source

3. What sort of actions/acting would a performer enact in the performance space?

Source	

4. How would a performer use their voice?

Source	

5. What objects (props/costume/set/puppets) might a performer manipulate?

Source	

6. What set would be used?

| Source | |

7. What costume would be used?

| Source | |

8. What prop(s) would be used?

| Source | |

9. How would lighting be used?

Source

10. What sound and/or music would be used?

Source

11. Are there any other distinguishing features?

Source

Activity

Aspect(s) of theory mood board

Building on the work you did in the previous exercise, this activity will help you to begin practically exploring how the chosen aspect(s) of theory might be brought to life.

- Use all your research to create six physical images with your body or capture a recording of your voice demonstrating how your chosen aspect(s) of theatre theory might look or sound like in action. If your aspect(s) of theory is focused on production elements, you can either use any available production resources or set them up in miniature using small models of sets, torches, pre-recorded sound effects, and so on.

- Record your images/sound by taking six photographs or audio recordings of yourself physicalizing (through body/voice) the aspect(s) of theory, showing it through performance or production elements or through a combination of both. The photographs or audio recordings may show the aspect(s) of theory in its entirety or focus on a detail.

- Collate these images/recordings digitally to create an aspect(s) of theory mood board.

- Work with a partner. Present your mood board explaining the chosen aspect(s) of theory and what it might look like in practice through elements of performance and production.

There are many ways of exploring an aspect(s) of theory, be it through games, activities, rehearsal processes, observations or mini performances. The next activity encourages you to play, experiment and work practically with aspects of your chosen theatre theory. This will help you develop your solo theatre piece.

Activity

Exploring aspect(s) of theory

- Choose six key quotes related to an aspect(s) of your chosen theatre theorist's theory (three from primary sources and from three from secondary sources).

- Complete the tables provided opposite. Alongside each quote create, develop or adapt an existing theatre activity or exercise that would give you the opportunity to practically explore the aspect(s) of the theory. In some instances, you might want to see if there are exercises or activities that have been developed by the theatre theorist themself.

- Once you have developed the activities, try them out.

- Having explored the aspect(s) of theory practically, create a one-minute solo performance to introduce the aspect(s) to a partner. Your performance should begin with "My name is [your name] and this is my version of an aspect(s) of [theorist's name] theory, exploring [aspect(s) of theory] in order to [theorist's intention]". For example, "My name is Sofia and this is my version of an aspect of Lepage's theory, exploring the use of projections in order to transport the audience to another world".

- Record your one-minute performance on video.

- Watch your performance and identify which aspect(s) of theatre theory you think are clearly communicated and which may be unclear to others.

- Present your mini performance to your partner and get feedback regarding how clear the aspect(s) was and whether it managed to achieve its intention.

- Use this feedback to further develop your exploration of your selected aspect(s) of theory.

6.3 Developing theatre-maker intentions

In the solo theatre piece assessment task, your theatre-maker intentions must be aligned with the theatre theorist's overall intentions. This is to ensure that the aspect(s) of theory you explore is positioned firmly within a theorist's broader theatrical intentions. This should also provide clarity regarding the sort of effect the aspect(s) of theory should have on an audience. After all, it would be difficult for you to demonstrate an understanding of a theorist whose intention is to provide light entertainment by creating a piece of theatre that is politically provocative and requires the audience to think deeply and intellectually about particular issues.

Developing practical exercises or activities

Aspect of theory	Theorist's intention	Primary source	Activity/Exercise

Aspect of theory	Theorist's intention	Secondary source	Activity/Exercise

What the guide says

Theatre-maker intentions

Early on in the process students are required to formulate theatre-maker intentions for the solo performance. These defined intentions should clearly articulate what will be performed and the effect each student intends their piece to have on an audience.

Each student's theatre-maker intentions should be aligned with:
- the theatre theorist's overarching intentions (which may be theatrical, social, political, philosophical and so on)
- the purpose of these intentions regarding the effect the theorist wishes their theatre to have on the audience.

Here are some examples of possible intentions and theatre pieces developed for each of the example theatre theorists.

Theorist: Anne Bogart
Aspect(s) of theory: Space and time

Potential theatre-maker intentions	Potential theatre piece
Create audience awareness of the banality of beauty and how the passage of time is inevitable and pervasive.	Solo presentation of an original piece of theatre based on Shakespeare's *Sonnet 60*. Exploring time/tempo through repetition, and space through gesture and spatial relationships. Directed and performed by the student with a floor cloth designed and painted by the student.

Theorist: Robert Lepage
Aspect(s) of theory: Film projection

Potential theatre-maker intentions	Potential theatre piece
Immerse the audience in an experience of the senses, to make them feel what it would mean to lose everything in life while seeing there is always "light at the end of the tunnel".	Solo theatre presentation of a monologue about a tsunami. Created, directed and performed by the student using film projection designed by the student.

Theorist: Zeami Motokiyo
Aspect(s) of theory: Quality of movement

Potential theatre-maker intentions	Potential theatre piece
Present to the audience an aesthetic piece where the poetry of movement will transmit the happiness of an encounter with the celestial or sublime.	Solo presentation of the dance from *Hagoromo* (The Feather Robe). Directed and performed by the student with costume designed by the student.

Theorist: Julie Taymor
Aspect(s) of theory: Use of puppets as a device for storytelling

Potential theatre-maker intentions	Potential theatre piece
Engage the audience with a well-known story/fable that will show the universal and inter-cultural quality of the human condition.	Solo presentation of one of Aesop's fables adapted for the stage. Directed and performed by the student using puppets.

Theorist: Robert Wilson
Aspect(s) of theory: Use of light

Potential theatre-maker intentions	Potential theatre piece
Create a piece that aims at stimulating the senses of the audience. The focus will be on power and how it affects those who have it.	Solo presentation of an original piece of theatre without words based on *Macbeth* by Shakespeare. Directed and performed by the student focusing on lighting, multimedia and body language.

Activity

Developing theatre-maker intentions aligned with the theorist
Continue working on your chosen theatre theorist and chosen aspect(s) of theatre theory from the previous exercise.
- Look back at the theorist's overarching intentions you defined in the previous exercise.
- Use the questions below/opposite/overleaf to define your own theatre-maker intentions for the development of **your own** piece of theatre informed by the aspect(s) of theatre theory.
- Use the answers to these questions to write a first draft of your theatre-maker intentions. Make sure you address the following.

☑ The performance style of the piece
☑ The type of material used for performance
☑ The performance space you will use
☑ The effect you want your piece to have on an audience
☑ The aesthetics—what the piece looks and sounds like—and the use of performance and production elements

1. What aspect(s) of theory will you be focusing on?

2. What effect do you want to have on the audience? What do you want them to remember/think/feel? How will you achieve this?

3. What type of performance space will you use? Draw a diagram of the space.

4. What performance style will be used? Why?

5. What production elements will be used? Why?

6. What other special features might you employ? Why?

Definition: Developing the piece

A practical process of applying the selected aspect(s) of your chosen theory and incorporating performance and/or production elements to create, design and rehearse a solo theatre piece in order to fulfil your stated theatre-maker intentions. The process of development will often involve identifying the performance style of your piece, experimenting with different types of material for your performance (such as existing text, original text, or rejecting the use of text entirely), working in your chosen performance space, combining different performance and production elements, and rehearsing the solo piece to ensure it achieves the overall effect you want to have on your audience. You will need to be able to look back at this process and explain how you developed the piece in section 2 of the solo theatre piece report.

6.4 Performance material and the process of developing the piece

One of the key decisions you will need to make is about the performance material you will use or create for your solo theatre piece. The *Theatre guide* states that you can use or adapt an existing text, create new text or not use any text. The performance material should be appropriate to the theorist and should help to make the aspect(s) of theatre theory you are exploring clear to an audience and to the examiner. It should be aligned with the theorist's overarching intentions and also help you to meet your own intentions.

The first thing to do is to see what sort of performance material the theorist themself has either used, worked on or created. Even if you do not use this, it will give you a sense of what sort of performance material the theorist is interested in.

Examples of different forms of performance material
Here are some feasible and creative approaches to sourcing or developing performance material.

- Using edited and collated pieces of existing performance material
- Transforming non-theatrical text into a performance text (for example, a newspaper article to present theatre theorist Augusto Boal's newspaper theatre)
- Generating original material written or devised by you
- Working with an existing piece of music
- Using a series of digital projections
- Using a transcript or film of action that does not use any words or sound (for example, to present theatre theorist Marcel Marceau's use of gesture)

The following are examples of the different forms of performance material that have been used by theorists and that you could use for your solo theatre piece.

➤ A published text or play text that is traditionally associated with the theatre theorist (for example, the stage production of *The Lion King* is associated with the work of theatre theorist Julie Taymor)

➤ A published play text written by the theatre theorist or their company (for example, theatre theorist Bertolt Brecht's *The Caucasian Chalk Circle*)

➤ A published text or play text that is not associated with a theorist but that can be used to show the aspect(s) of theory in action (for example, a Shakespearean monologue informed by theatre theorist Rudolf Laban's ideas of space harmony)

➤ A short story (for example, theatre theorist Steven Berkoff's adaptation of *The Fall of the House of Usher* by Edgar Allan Poe)

➤ A piece of non-fiction (for example, using Buddhist texts to present an aspect(s) of theatre theorist Zeami Motokiyo's theory)

> **Top tip**
> If you choose to use text for your solo theatre piece, this text can come from a variety of places. You might choose, for example, an existing play, a piece of poetry, some prose or an excerpt from a news article. Alternatively, it could be something entirely original.

Activity

Working with existing performance material

This activity focuses on the use of a play text as your chosen performance material in order to fulfil the theatre-maker intentions you identified in the previous activity. You can work with a partner or, if you are working on your own, imagine you are directing someone else. You should continue working on the chosen aspect(s) of theatre theory that you explored in the previous activities.

• Research and choose a piece(s) of performance material associated with—or appropriate to—your chosen theatre theorist. Choose material where you can apply the specific aspect(s) of theatre theory you have chosen. This can either be one section or except from a play text or taken from a collection of pieces, scenes or monologues. You are free to change or edit the text or put different pieces together in a text collage—whatever best serves your theatre-maker intentions.

• Prepare your performance text so that it is ready to be analysed and performed.

• Analyse the text and identify key themes and ideas or any other information that is important for staging the material.

• Imagine you will be directing another solo performer (this can be your partner or an imaginary performer). Think about your theatre-maker intentions, aligned with the theatre theorist's intentions and how these will be met in a performance.

• In box 1 overleaf, make notes and sketch drawings and/or diagrams to communicate how you would go about directing a performer in this piece, focusing on use of body, voice and positioning on stage. Remember, your aim is to meet the theatre-maker intentions you worked on in the previous activity.

• Thinking as a designer for this piece, think about the space and what production elements you might need. Communicate your vision for these in box 2 overleaf.

1. My approach to directing this piece

2. My approach to designing this piece

Working with existing performance material (continued)

- You are now going to work on staging the material. You can use your notes to either direct your partner or yourself. Begin by focusing specifically on the performer and what they are doing on stage even if your aspect(s) of theory is production focused. Try some of the following approaches to help you with the staging.

  - ☑ Break down the performance material moment by moment and apply the aspect(s) of theatre theory to it
  - ☑ Break down the aspect(s) of theatre theory and choose material to stage the aspect(s) of theory
  - ☑ Think of various techniques you can use to make the aspect(s) of theatre theory visible to an observer/audience/examiner and to fulfil your intentions

- Once you have experimented with how you might stage the material, direct your partner or yourself.
- Now consider the production elements. Depending on the aspect(s) of theory and the theorist, the production elements may be the focus of the piece or may be minimal.
- Try some of the following approaches to help you with the design.

  - ☑ Try working with the text in different spaces
  - ☑ Rehearse using any props/objects that might enhance the visibility of the aspect(s) of theatre theory and fulfil your intentions
  - ☑ Rehearse wearing clothing that might enhance the visibility of the aspect(s) of theatre theory and fulfil your intentions
  - ☑ Add sound/music to enhance the aspect(s) of theatre theory and fulfil your intentions
  - ☑ Add lights to enhance the aspect(s) of theatre theory and fulfil your intentions

- When you are happy with the performance and production elements, video record the piece. This will be very rough and is not by any means a finished piece. This is only to give you a sense of whether the aspect(s) is visible and/or your intentions are met.
- Watch the film and assess how visible the aspect(s) of theory is and whether you have fulfilled your intentions.
- At this point you may choose to adapt or change the performance material.
- Redraft your theatre-maker intentions in box 3 below, adding how you are using text and how this relates to your chosen aspect(s) of theory. Try to also include more explicit references to how performance and production elements will be used.

3. Redrafting my theatre-maker intentions

Working with original material

In this activity you will be creating your own material in order to demonstrate the aspect(s) of theory you are working with to an audience and to fulfil your theatre-maker intentions. Creating original material will be more appropriate for some aspect(s) of theory than others. This will often be the case when exploring theorists who are not text-based or who do not use text in a traditional way.

- Your task is to create a three-minute solo performance based on a starting point to demonstrate your aspect(s) of theory to an audience. You can create your own text or use no text at all. To begin, choose one of the following starting points.

  - ☑ A newspaper article
  - ☑ An image or photograph
  - ☑ A poem
  - ☑ An idea/theme/issue
  - ☑ An object
  - ☑ An event
  - ☑ A location
  - ☑ A filmed interview
  - ☑ A fairy tale

- Think about how you will transform the starting point you have selected into a three-minute solo performance that will demonstrate your aspect(s) of theory to an audience.
- Record your ideas in the spaces provided below/opposite.

Ideas of what the piece will be about

Performance space

Elements of performance	Elements of production (set, costume, props, lights, sound)

Activity

Working with original material (continued)

- Use the ideas you have captured to stage your piece focusing only on performance elements. Once you feel your performance is ready, film yourself performing the piece without any production elements.
- Watch the recording of the piece and decide on which production elements you will now use and how these will be used to make your chosen aspect(s) of theory more visible and to fulfil your intentions. If you decide not to use any or very few production elements, you need to come up with a justification for this.
- Add the production elements and film the piece again.
- Watch the two video recordings and analyse how the aspect(s) of theatre theory was made visible and how your theatre-maker intentions were met through a) performance elements and b) production elements.
- In box 4 below, redraft your theatre-maker intentions once again adding the performance material. Try to also include more explicit references to how performance and production elements will be used.

Reflection point
Reflect on how you approached making the aspect of theatre theory visible in your performances, the challenges you faced and how you addressed these. How did performance elements enhance the visibility of the chosen aspect of theory? How did production elements enhance the visibility of the chosen aspect of theory? Did you prefer working with existing text or working with a starting point?

4. Redrafting my theatre-maker intentions

Activity

Recording the process of development

It is important to keep a record of how your solo theatre piece has been developed, staged, rehearsed, designed, and prepared for presentation to an audience. The following tasks encourage you to explain the process of creating and developing your solo piece to someone outside your class. Think about how you would get someone to really understand how a solo piece of theatre based on an aspect(s) of theatre theory is created and produced.

- Think of the making of the solo theatre piece as a personal story that begins with a theorist's words and ends with a solo theatre piece that you have created, designed, directed and performed. If this story was written in five parts, what would be the title of each part? Use the space below to record each title.
- If this story was a film, what would be the five images that would best illustrate each part of it? Sketch these in the storyboard space provided below.
- Create a diagram (a visual) in the space opposite that would go on a classroom wall informing younger theatre students about the process of making solo theatre work based on an aspect(s) of theatre theory.

The making of the solo theatre piece: Chapter titles	
1	
2	
3	
4	
5	

The making of the solo theatre piece: Storyboard images		
1	2	3
4	5	

The making of the solo theatre piece: Classroom wall visual

6.5 Feedback and evaluation

Collecting feedback and using this to develop your solo theatre piece is an essential part of the process of creating a solo performance. Working solo makes it difficult to look at your work objectively, especially because you are the director, designer, and performer. You can be so involved in the task that you might not realise if your chosen aspect(s) of theory is unclear to the audience or to the examiner.

Feedback from an audience is a requirement of the solo theatre piece assessment task. This is not feedback designed to help you to develop your work but rather feedback after your final performance that gives you information regarding how the audience received your solo piece. This feedback is needed as evidence in your assessment task to inform you of:

- the extent to which your chosen aspect(s) of theatre theory is evident to the audience
- whether your (and the theatre theorist's) intentions have been met.

It is important, therefore, that anyone giving feedback should understand your intentions, have an overview of your chosen theorist and the chosen aspect(s) of theory. Without this information, it would be difficult for them to give you feedback that will help you meet the requirements of the assessment task. Here are some ideas on how you can make sure your audience is appropriately informed.

The informed spectator

Select an informed audience
The work is presented to an audience that is familiar with the theorist, your chosen aspect(s) of theory and your theatre-maker intentions.

Use publicity material
The theorist, your chosen aspect(s) of theory and your theatre-maker intentions are publicized in any marketing material.

Send information in advance
Information regarding the theorist, your chosen aspect(s) of theory and your theatre-maker intentions is communicated in advance to the audience.

Displays
The theorist, your chosen aspect(s) of theory and your theatre-maker intentions are communicated through information posted in the foyer or in the performance space.

Pre-show
The theorist, your chosen aspect(s) of theory and your theatre-maker intentions are communicated to the audience before the piece begins. This could be through a video or audio playing in the foyer.

Programme notes
Information regarding the theorist, your chosen aspect(s) of theory and your theatre-maker intentions is explained in programme notes or in notes handed to each audience member.

Introductory presentation
The audience are given a presentation explaining the theorist, your chosen aspect(s) of theory and your theatre-maker intentions before the piece is performed.

Presentation after the piece
The audience is given a presentation explaining the theorist, your chosen aspect(s) of theory and your theatre-maker intentions after the piece has been performed. This can happen before a talkback or before any feedback is collected.

Gathering and recording feedback

One area that you need to think about is how you will **gather** and **record** feedback that will be most useful for your evaluation in order to meet the criteria of the assessment task.

Think about the following ways of gathering feedback after the performance. Which do you think is the most effective? Which would you find most beneficial?

- Choosing someone else to chair a feedback session and ask questions while you observe
- Audio or video record the feedback session
- Give the audience questionnaires to fill in immediately after the performance
- Set up a digital space where feedback can be posted by the audience
- Create a survey to send to the audience to be completed digitally
- Create a feedback space—this can be a wall, table or other surface where the audience writes responses
- Gather short bursts of feedback in the form of vox pops—recording feedback at random from individuals and capturing it either as audio or as video

Getting the information you need for your solo theatre piece report means asking the right questions. The best type of questions are open ones which require more than a yes or no answer.

Think of feedback as being three types of question.

- **Holistic questions** are ones that ask about the whole piece (e.g. What did you think I was trying to communicate in my solo theatre piece?).
- **Particular questions** are ones that focus on a particular moment or element (e.g. Why did you think I used a blue light at the opening of the piece?).
- **Competency questions** are ones that ask about the extent to which something was achieved or the level of a skill (e.g. How effective was my use of voice?).

Activity

Asking the right questions

- Using your theatre journal, write one holistic, one particular and one competency question for each of the following areas. This will give you a bank of nine questions to ask your audience.

  ☑ The effectiveness of your piece regarding your use of elements of performance and production
  ☑ The extent to which you met your intentions
  ☑ The extent to which your chosen aspect(s) of theory was discernible

Activity

Reflection and evaluation

Self-reflection and evaluation are important skills for all theatre-makers as they offer a process that helps you to develop as an artist. They also help you to develop your skills and encourage you, in this area of the theatre course, to consider the effectiveness of a piece of theatre you have been wholly responsible for. Reflection and evaluation also provide you with the perfect opportunity to think about the purpose of theatre theory and how it can be used to inform theatre-making.

- Think about one of the pieces you created in the previous activities in this chapter.
- Use the diagram below to evaluate yourself in the various roles of creator, designer, director and performer of the piece your performed based on theatre theory.
- Complete the self-evaluation box opposite, explaining the extent to which you think you met your theatre-maker intentions.
- Referring to the notes you have written in the self-evaluation box, record an audio track explaining each of the following.

  ☑ How effective your piece was with regard to the use of performance and production elements
  ☑ The extent to which you think you met your theatre-maker intentions
  ☑ The extent to which your chosen aspect(s) of theory was discernible in the piece

How effective were each of the following areas in your chosen piece?

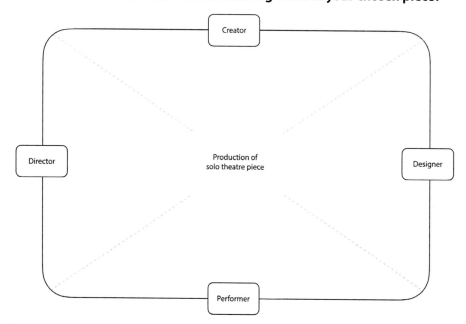

Self-evaluation

To what extent do you think you met your theatre-maker intentions?

6.6 Preparing for assessment: Structuring your report and recording your performance

For the assessment of this task, you will need to submit a report—that must also include a list of all the primary and secondary sources you have cited in your work—and a video recording of your performed solo theatre piece (4–7 minutes).

The report
The report should be written in the first person and present your:

- research
- theatre-maker intentions
- evaluation of the finished theatre piece.

Definition: Report
A report is something written after something has happened. It looks back at what has happened and draws conclusions from it.

The word limit for the report is 2,500 words maximum, which includes all labels, quotations and citations. This word limit does not include the list of sources used. The report is assessed on-screen and you must ensure that the work is clear and legible when presented in a digital, on-screen format.

You need to structure your report carefully to ensure you address the criteria weighting for each area. Your completed report should adhere to the following structure.

Structuring your report

1. **Researching theatre theory** (8 marks)
   With reference to their research, each student explains the chosen theory with a focus on the theorist's overarching intentions and the selected aspect(s) of the theory. References to research should support the student's explanation of both the theory and aspect(s) chosen, as examiners are interested in ensuring the student's research is upheld and framed by pertinent evidence from the primary and secondary sources explored.

   Recommended maximum number of words: 1,000

2. **Developing the piece** (4 marks)
   Each student presents their defined and clearly articulated theatre-maker intentions for the solo theatre piece and explains the process of developing the solo theatre piece, as informed by their chosen theory, through the use of performance and production elements.

   Recommended maximum number of words: 750 words

3. **Evaluating the performance** (4 marks)
   Each student evaluates the presented solo theatre piece, explaining the extent to which their intentions were fulfilled and considering the feedback received from the audience.

   Recommended maximum number of words: 750 words

Use of images and other visual material
You can include carefully selected visuals in your report, where directly relevant to, or helpful for, your explanation. This might include your own photographs, images or scans. Make sure they are of an appropriate quality. All images must be clearly labelled and appropriately referenced to acknowledge the source, following the protocol of the referencing style chosen by your school. The labelling of the images is included in the final word limit of the report and should contain the minimum information to ensure the examiner understands the significance of the images.

Video recording
Your entire solo theatre piece will need to be video recorded and submitted for assessment. The performance must last between four and seven minutes. The *Theatre guide* states the following about the video recording.

What the guide says

- The full performance of the solo theatre piece must be captured in a video recording that is submitted for assessment. This must be a continuous, single-camera, unedited record and must capture the full presentation of the piece from the best vantage point possible. The video recording device must not be switched off during the performance.

- As each student will be assessed on the use of theatre-maker skills and techniques to deliver the solo theatre piece, it is crucial that all action can be clearly seen and heard in the recording. The video recording device may pan and zoom in order to capture as much of the live action as possible and it is permitted to use close-ups for moments that have been pre-determined by the student.

- During the assessment task the teacher should assist with video recording the solo theatre piece to ensure it accurately captures the assessment task. In preparing to video record the assessed solo theatre piece teachers are encouraged to allow students time to walk through their performance prior to filming to give the operator of the video recording device an indication of how the space will be used and the most appropriate way of framing each section.

Solo theatre piece assessment criteria

The assessment criteria for the solo theatre piece are as follows.

Solo theatre piece assessment criteria

A: Researching theatre theory

Evidence: report and list of sources

   i. With specific references to their research, to what extent does the student explain their chosen theatre theory with a focus on the theorist's overarching intentions?

  ii. With specific references to their research, to what extent does the student explain the chosen aspect(s) of the theatre theory?

What the examiner wants to see

Criterion A(i)

- That you explain and show, with reference to your research, that you have understood the theorist's theories and the nature of their theatre practice
- That you explain and show, with reference to your research, that you have understood the overarching intentions of the theorist
- That you have consulted both primary and secondary sources

Criterion A(ii)

- That you have chosen an aspect(s) of theatre theory
- That you explain and show, with reference to your research, that you have understood your chosen aspect(s) of theatre theory

> **Solo theatre piece assessment criteria**
> **B: Reflecting on the performed solo theatre piece**
> Evidence: report and list of sources
>
> i. With reference to their theatre-maker intentions, to what extent does the student explain the process of developing the solo theatre piece, as informed by their chosen theory?
> ii. With reference to audience feedback, to what extent does the student evaluate the effectiveness of the presented solo theatre piece, explaining the extent to which the piece fulfilled its intentions?

What the examiner wants to see
Criterion B(i)
- That you have developed theatre-maker intentions
- That you explain the process of how you developed your solo theatre piece with reference to your theatre-maker intentions
- That you explain how the application of your chosen aspect(s) to your solo theatre piece has informed how you developed the piece

Criterion B(ii)
- That you evaluate the effectiveness of your solo theatre piece
- That you refer to audience feedback regarding the effectiveness of your solo theatre piece
- That you explain the extent to which you met your theatre-maker intentions

> **Solo theatre piece assessment criteria**
> **C: Theatre theory in performance**
> Evidence: video recording
>
> i. To what extent are the selected aspect(s) of theatre theory applied in the solo theatre piece?
> ii. To what extent does the student use performance and/or production elements effectively in the solo theatre piece to fulfil their intentions?

What the examiner wants to see
Criterion C(i)
- That you have used an aspect(s) of theory in your piece of theatre in such a way that it is visible to the examiner
- That your theatre piece shows that you have understood your chosen aspect(s) of theory and the theorist's overarching intentions

Criterion C(ii)
- That you have fulfilled your intentions
- That you have used performance and/or production elements effectively to fulfil your intentions

Chapter 6: Recap

In this chapter we have explored the topic of performing theatre theory and the solo theatre piece, focusing on:

- choosing a theatre theorist

- researching their theories and their overarching intentions

- selecting and researching an aspect(s) of theatre theory

- practically exploring an aspect(s) of theatre theory

- developing theatre-maker intentions that are aligned with the theorist's overarching intentions

- choosing existing performance material for the creation of a solo theatre piece

- creating original performance material for the creation of a solo theatre piece

- preparing a solo theatre piece for an audience that applies your chosen aspect(s) of theory

- considering the use of performance and production elements

- evaluating the effectiveness of your solo theatre piece

- capturing and recording audience feedback

- structuring your report and recording your performance for assessment.

Appendix 1: Assessment criteria—production proposal (IA)

A: Ideas and intentions
Evidence: production proposal

i. To what extent does the student explain the ideas addressed by the chosen play text, with reference to the play text?
ii. To what extent does the student explain their intentions for the staging of the entire play?

Marks	
1-2	i. The student lists the ideas presented in the chosen play text. ii. The student lists their intentions for the staging of the entire play.
3-4	i. The student outlines the ideas presented in the chosen play text with reference to the play text. ii. The student outlines their intentions for the staging of the entire play.
5-6	i. The student describes the ideas presented in the chosen play text with reference to the play text. ii. The student describes their intentions for the staging of the entire play.
7-8	i. The student explains the ideas presented in the chosen play text, with reference to the play text. ii. The student explains their intentions for the staging of the entire play.

B: The proposed design
Evidence: production proposal

i. To what extent does the student present their visual production design ideas with an explanation of how these will be used to achieve their intentions in the staging of the entire play?

Mark	
1	i. The student presents their visual production design ideas with a list of information regarding how production elements will be used.
2	i. The student presents their visual production design ideas with an outline of how production elements will be used to achieve their intentions.
3	i. The student presents their visual production design ideas with a description of how production elements will be used to achieve their intentions.
4	i. The student presents their visual production design ideas with an explanation of how production elements will be used to achieve their intentions.

C: The proposed staging of one moment of the play
Evidence: production proposal

i. To what extent does the student explain how they would use performance elements to effectively create tension, emotion, atmosphere and/or meaning ("TEAM") in one specific moment they have chosen to stage?
ii. To what extent does the student explain how they would use production elements to effectively create tension, emotion, atmosphere and/or meaning ("TEAM") in one specific moment they have chosen to stage?

Marks	
1-2	i. The student lists how they would use performance elements to create tension, emotion, atmosphere and/or meaning ("TEAM") in the moment they have chosen to stage. ii. The student lists how they would use production elements to create tension, emotion, atmosphere and/or meaning ("TEAM") in the moment they have chosen to stage.
3-4	i. The student outlines how they would use performance elements to create tension, emotion, atmosphere and/or meaning ("TEAM") in the moment they have chosen to stage. ii. The student outlines how they would use production elements to create tension, emotion, atmosphere and/or meaning ("TEAM") in the moment they have chosen to stage.
5-6	i. The student describes how they would use performance elements to create tension, emotion, atmosphere and/or meaning ("TEAM") in the moment they have chosen to stage. ii. The student describes how they would use production elements to create tension, emotion, atmosphere and/or meaning ("TEAM") in the moment they have chosen to stage.
7-8	i. The student explains how they would use performance elements to effectively create tension, emotion, atmosphere and/or meaning ("TEAM") in the moment they have chosen to stage. ii. The student explains how they would use production elements to effectively create tension, emotion, atmosphere and/or meaning ("TEAM") in the moment they have chosen to stage.

Possible characteristics

Marks	Level	Characteristics
1-2	Limited	Irrelevant, Simplistic, Superficial
3-4	Adequate	Attempted, Underdeveloped, Uneven
5-6	Good	Accurate, Focused, Relevant
7-8	Excellent	Discerning, Insightful, Thorough

Appendix 2: Assessment criteria—research presentation

A: The unfamiliar theatre tradition
Evidence: video recording and list of sources and resources

i. With specific references to their research, to what extent does the student explain the unfamiliar theatre tradition they have chosen to explore?

ii. With specific references to their research, to what extent does the student explain the performance convention they have chosen to explore?

Students who do not select a theatre tradition from the prescribed list will not be awarded a mark higher than 2 in this criterion

B: Practical exploration of the performance convention
Evidence: video recording and list of sources and resources

i. To what extent does the student demonstrate their process of practical exploration of the performance convention, in order to develop an understanding of the performance convention through the body and/or voice?

ii. To what extent does the student physically demonstrate how they have **experimented** with applying the performance convention to traditional performance material?

C: Reflection on learning
Evidence: video recording and list of sources and resources

i. To what extent does the student explain how their practical exploration of the performance convention has contributed to their continuing development as a performer?

ii. To what extent does the student explain how their inquiry into the chosen theatre tradition has further developed their understanding of theatre in the world?

	A: The unfamiliar theatre tradition	B: Practical exploration of the performance convention	C: Reflection on learning	Possible characteristics
1–2	i. The student lists features of the unfamiliar theatre tradition they have chosen to explore. ii. The student lists features of the performance convention they have chosen to explore.	i. The student demonstrates a limited process of practical exploration of the performance convention. ii. The student demonstrates in a limited way how they **applied** with applying the performance convention to traditional performance material, or uses material that is inappropriate to the tradition.	i. The student lists how they would use performance elements to create tension, emotion, atmosphere and/or meaning ("TEAM") in the moment they have chosen to stage. ii. The student lists how they would use production elements to create tension, emotion, atmosphere and/or meaning ("TEAM") in the moment they have chosen to stage.	***Limited*** *Irrelevant* *Simplistic* *Superficial*
3–4	i. With specific references to their research, the student outlines the unfamiliar theatre tradition they have chosen to explore. ii. With specific references to their research, the student outlines the performance convention they have chosen to explore.	i. The student demonstrates a moderate process of practical exploration of the performance convention. ii. The student moderately demonstrates how they have **experimented** with applying the performance convention to traditional performance material.	i. The student outlines how they would use performance elements to create tension, emotion, atmosphere and/or meaning ("TEAM") in the moment they have chosen to stage. ii. The student outlines how they would use production elements to create tension, emotion, atmosphere and/or meaning ("TEAM") in the moment they have chosen to stage.	***Adequate*** *Attempted* *Underdeveloped* *Uneven*
5–6	i. With specific references to their research, the student describes the unfamiliar theatre tradition they have chosen to explore. ii. With specific references to their research, the student describes the performance convention they have chosen to explore.	i. The student demonstrates a competent process of practical exploration of the performance convention. ii. The student competently demonstrates how they have **experimented** with applying the performance convention to traditional performance material.	i. The student describes how they would use performance elements to create tension, emotion, atmosphere and/or meaning ("TEAM") in the moment they have chosen to stage. ii. The student describes how they would use production elements to create tension, emotion, atmosphere and/or meaning ("TEAM") in the moment they have chosen to stage.	***Good*** *Accurate* *Focused* *Relevant*
7–8	i. With specific references to their research, the student explains the unfamiliar theatre tradition they have chosen to explore. ii. With specific references to their research, the student explains the performance convention they have chosen to explore.	i. The student demonstrates an effective process of practical exploration of the performance convention. ii. The student effectively demonstrates how they have **experimented** with applying the performance convention to traditional performance material.	i. The student explains how they would use performance elements to effectively create tension, emotion, atmosphere and/or meaning ("TEAM") in the moment they have chosen to stage. ii. The student explains how they would use production elements to create tension, emotion, atmosphere and/or meaning ("TEAM") in the moment they have chosen to stage.	***Excellent*** *Discerning* *Insightful* *Thorough*

Appendix 3: Assessment criteria—collaborative project

A: The collaborative creative process and performance
Evidence: cover sheet, project report and list of sources

i. With reference to significant instances from the process, to what extent does the student explain how they consider the piece was collaboratively created by the ensemble?

ii. With reference to audience feedback, to what extent does the student evaluate the effectiveness of the final piece as a whole, in relation to how they consider the ensemble's intentions were achieved?

B: Individual contributions to the performance
Evidence: cover sheet, project report and list of sources

i. To what extent does the student explain how they used their performance skills (body and/or voice) to effectively contribute to one moment of tension, emotion, atmosphere and/or meaning ("TEAM") visible in the video recording?

ii. To what extent does the student explain how their specific individual artistic contribution(s) to the development and staging of the piece as creator, designer and/or director effectively contributed to the fulfilment of the ensemble's intentions in one moment seen in the video recording?

C: Effectiveness of individual contributions seen in the video recording
Evidence: cover sheet and video recording

i. To what extent do the student's performance skills (body and/or voice) effectively contribute to a moment of tension, emotion, atmosphere and/or meaning ("TEAM") seen in the video recording (as specified by the student in section 2(a) of the project report)?

ii. To what extent do the student's own individual contributions to the artistic development and/or staging of the piece as creator, designer and/or director (as specified by the student in section 2(b) of the project report) effectively contribute to the fulfilment of the ensemble's intentions within the context of the whole video recording?

Marks	Possible characteristics	A: The collaborative creative process and performance	B: Individual contributions to the performance	C: Effectiveness of individual contributions seen in the video recording
1–2	**Limited** *Irrelevant* *Simplistic* *Superficial*	i. The student lists the ways in which they consider the piece was collaboratively created by the ensemble. ii. The student comments on the effectiveness of the final piece as a whole, listing the ways in which they consider the ensemble's intentions were achieved.	i. The student lists the ways in which they used their performance skills (body and/or voice) to effectively contribute to one moment of tension, emotion, atmosphere and/or meaning ("TEAM") visible in the video recording. ii. The student lists how their own specific individual artistic contribution(s) to the development and/or staging of the piece as creator, designer and/or director.	i. The student's use of performance skills (body and/or voice) makes a limited contribution to the specified moment of tension, emotion, atmosphere and/or meaning ("TEAM") seen in the video recording. ii. The student's specified contributions to the artistic development and/or staging of the piece make a limited contribution to the fulfilment of the ensemble's intentions within the context of the whole video recording.
3–4	**Adequate** *Attempted* *Underdeveloped* *Uneven*	i. With reference to significant instances from the process, the student outlines how they consider the piece was collaboratively created by the ensemble. ii. With reference to audience feedback, the student considers the effectiveness of the final piece as a whole, in relation to how they consider the ensemble's intentions were achieved.	i. The student outlines how they used their performance skills (body and/or voice) to effectively contribute to one moment of tension, emotion, atmosphere and/or meaning ("TEAM") visible in the video recording. ii. The student outlines how their own specific individual artistic contribution(s) to the development and/or staging of the piece as creator, designer and/or director effectively contributed to the fulfilment of the ensemble's intentions in one moment seen in the video recording.	i. The student uses their performance skills (body and/or voice) to moderately contribute to the specified moment of tension, emotion, atmosphere and/or meaning ("TEAM") seen in the video recording. ii. The student's specified contributions to the artistic development and/or staging of the piece moderately contribute to the fulfilment of the ensemble's intentions within the context of the whole video recording.
5–6	**Good** *Accurate* *Focused* *Relevant*	i. With reference to significant instances from the process, the student describes how they consider the piece was collaboratively created by the ensemble. ii. With reference to audience feedback, the student appraises the effectiveness of the final piece as a whole, in relation to how they consider the ensemble's intentions were achieved.	i. The student describes how they used their performance skills (body and/or voice) to effectively contribute to one moment of tension, emotion, atmosphere and/or meaning ("TEAM") visible in the video recording. ii. The student describes how their own specific individual artistic contribution(s) to the development and/or staging of the piece as creator, designer and/or director effectively contributed to the fulfilment of the ensemble's intentions in one moment seen in the video recording.	i. The student uses their performance skills (body and/or voice) to competently contribute to the specified moment of tension, emotion, atmosphere and/or meaning ("TEAM") seen in the video recording. ii. The student's specified contributions to the artistic development and/or staging of the piece competently contribute to fulfilment of the ensemble's intentions within the context of the whole video recording.
7–8	**Excellent** *Discerning* *Insightful* *Thorough*	i. With reference to significant instances from the process, the student explains how they consider the piece was collaboratively created by the ensemble. ii. With reference to audience feedback, the student evaluates the effectiveness of the final piece as a whole, in relation to how they consider the ensemble's intentions were achieved.	i. The student explains how they used their performance skills (body and/or voice) to effectively contribute to one moment of tension, emotion, atmosphere and/or meaning ("TEAM") visible in the video recording. ii. The student explains how their own specific individual artistic contribution(s) to the development and/or staging of the piece as creator, designer and/or director effectively contributed to the fulfilment of the ensemble's intentions in one moment seen in the video recording.	i. The student uses their performance skills (body and/or voice) to effectively contribute to the specified moment of tension, emotion, atmosphere and/or meaning ("TEAM") seen in the video recording. ii. The student's specified contributions to the artistic development and/or staging of the piece effectively contribute to the fulfilment of the ensemble's intentions within the context of the whole video recording.

Appendix 4: Assessment criteria—solo theatre piece (HL only)

A: Researching theatre theory
Evidence: report and list of sources

i. With specific references to their research, to what extent does the student explain their chosen theatre theory with a focus on the theorist's overarching intentions?
ii. With specific references to their research, to what extent does the student explain the chosen aspect(s) of the theatre theory?

B: Reflecting on the performed solo theatre piece
Evidence: report and list of sources

i. With reference to their theatre-maker intentions, to what extent does the student explain the process of having developed the solo theatre piece, as informed by their chosen theory?
ii. With reference to audience feedback, to what extent does the student evaluate the effectiveness of the presented solo theatre piece, explaining the extent to which the piece fulfilled its intentions?

C: Theatre theory in performance
Evidence: video recording

i. To what extent are the selected aspect(s) of theatre theory applied in the solo theatre piece?
ii. To what extent does the student use performance and/or production elements effectively in the solo theatre piece to fulfil their intentions?

Possible characteristics	A: Researching theatre theory	B: Reflecting on the performed solo theatre piece	C: Theatre theory in performance
Limited — Irrelevant, Simplistic, Superficial (1–2)	i. The student lists features of the theatre theory. ii. The student lists features of the chosen aspect(s) of the theatre theory.	i. The student lists the process of developing the solo theatre piece, as informed by their chosen theory. ii. The student comments on the effectiveness of the presented solo theatre piece, listing the ways in which their theatre-maker intentions were achieved.	i. The application of the selected aspect(s) of theatre theory in the solo theatre piece is limited. ii. The student's use of performance and/or production elements in the solo theatre piece is limited.
Adequate — Attempted, Underdeveloped, Uneven (3–4)	i. With specific references to their research, the student outlines the chosen theatre theory with a focus on the theorist's overarching intentions. ii. With specific references to their research, the student outlines the chosen aspect(s) of the theatre theory.	i. With reference to their theatre-maker intentions, the student outlines the process of developing the solo theatre piece, as informed by their chosen theory. ii. The student considers the effectiveness of the presented solo theatre piece, outlining the extent to which their theatre-maker intentions were achieved. References to audience feedback are mostly appropriate.	i. The application of the selected aspect(s) of theatre theory in the solo theatre piece is moderate. ii. The student's use of performance and/or production elements in the solo theatre piece to fulfil their intentions is moderate.
Good — Accurate, Focused, Relevant (5–6)	i. With specific references to their research, the student describes the chosen theatre theory with a focus on the theorist's overarching intentions. ii. With specific references to their research, the student describes the chosen aspect(s) of the theatre theory.	i. With reference to their theatre-maker intentions, the student describes the process of developing the solo theatre piece, as informed by their chosen theory. ii. The student appraises the effectiveness of the presented solo theatre piece, describing the extent to which their theatre-maker intentions were achieved. References to audience feedback are relevant.	i. The application of the selected aspect(s) of theatre theory in the solo theatre piece is competent. ii. The student's use of performance and/or production elements in the solo theatre piece to fulfil their intentions is competent.
Excellent — Discerning, Insightful, Thorough (7–8)	i. With specific references to their research, the student explains the chosen theatre theory with a focus on the theorist's overarching intentions. ii. With specific references to their research, the student explains the chosen aspect(s) of the theatre theory.	i. With reference to their theatre-maker intentions, the student explains the process of developing the solo theatre piece, as informed by their chosen theory. ii. The student evaluates the effectiveness of the presented solo theatre piece, explaining the extent to which their theatre-maker intentions were achieved. References to audience feedback effectively support the student's evaluation.	i. The application of the selected aspect(s) of theatre theory in the solo theatre piece is effective. ii. The student's use of performance and/or production elements in the solo theatre piece to fulfil their intentions is effective.